RECONCILED WITH GOD

RECONCILED
WITH GOD

by B.-M. CHEVIGNARD, O. P.

translated by Angèle Demand

SHEED AND WARD : NEW YORK

© Sheed and Ward, Inc., 1967

This book was originally published in French under the title Réconciliés avec Dieu, © 1965, by les Éditions du Cerf, Paris.

Library of Congress Catalog Card Number 67-21906

Nihil Obstat:
   Rt. Rev. Msgr. James T. Clarke
   Censor Deputatus
   July 15, 1967

Imprimatur:
   ✠ Most Rev. J. Carroll McCormick
   Bishop of Scranton
   July 15, 1967

The Bible text in this publication is from the Revised Standard Version of the Bible, copyrighted 1946 and 1952 by the Division of Christian Education of the National Council of Churches, and used by permission.

Manufactured in the United States of America

Contents

Foreword

One of the great truths on which the Second Vatican Council threw new light is the unity baptism brings to all the People of God: the Church is founded on baptism and from it she derives her holiness and mystery and her universal mission.

I wrote this book with the idea of giving Christians involved in the world a better understanding of what their baptism means as the source of the grace flowing in them, so that they might better understand the urgency of their mission to bear witness to God and Christ in the world.

It is not a formally ordered book.[1] Its value—if it is found to have any—will be in its informal working out of the way in which we should be nourished at the deepest and simplest sources of Christian life: the word of God and our baptism— the new birth which, now as always, brings forth saints and witnesses to Christ.

[1] Several chapters of this book appeared originally in *Cahiers St. Dominique*, a magazine for Dominican Tertiaries.

RECONCILED WITH GOD

Part I

HOLINESS OF THE BAPTIZED

1. Introduction:
God Makes Saints Everywhere

There is one supernatural experience about which ordained priests agree—namely, that God is supremely free; he calls whom he will; he makes saints everywhere. Where did these priests find the greatest examples of devotion, courage and silent love, the greatest capacity for sacrifice? Not necessarily in the cloisters, however great the fervor there. Priests love to discover with sober joy the evidence that lay people too are called to holiness. And they see no wonder in this. For is it not God who makes his saints? To him alone be honor and glory.

The doctrinal reason for this truth of experience is easy to understand: let us recall it briefly. "There is one body and one Spirit, just as you were called to the one hope that belongs to your call, one Lord, one faith, one baptism, one God and Father of us all, who is above all and through all and in all" (Ep. 4.4–6).

Thus the plan of God is a unity, and so is the race of Christians all born of the same baptism. It is the grace of baptism that makes saints, and everything begins to germinate at this depth. Indeed, the differences due to our particular vocations, to our different states of life, are considerable, but they remain accidental in relation to our fundamental unity in Christ.

Priests, religious, parents, single men and women living in the world—we are all fundamentally in communion through our common baptism. Transcending our differences without denying them, we are united at a deeper level as disciples of Christ. Two followers of Christ, one a priest, the other the head of a family, meet. They recognize and love each other. They share the same faith, the same hope, the same baptism. God can make them both saints. "There is but one body and one Spirit."

St. Thomas Aquinas strongly emphasized this unity of Christian grace. In his moral theology he develops in hundreds of articles what he calls "the grace of the Holy Spirit"—later called "grace of the virtues and gifts." There are not two sanctifying graces, that of the saints and that of the "ordinary Christians." There is but one: the grace which, coming from God himself, makes us sons of God in Christ, and which, by its very nature, leads to him. In all of us grace unfolds in the virtues—the hidden, infused energies of the soul—activating the gifts of the Holy Spirit, which endow the soul with a certain docility to God. Thus every Christian is "spiritual" by birth, from the time of his baptism. There are not "spiritual Christians" on one hand and "ordinary Christians" on the other. There are only Christians, all of them frail human beings, but called by God to become spiritual through him. The ways of the Lord are without number. He makes light of our classifications. He calls whom he will—poor, rich, ignorant, cultured, adult, child, priest, lay person—and the holiest will be the one who has listened to his word the most attentively and followed him with the closest fidelity. God's priests are witnesses to this, and they rejoice in declaring that God is God, and that he makes his saints everywhere.

One always hesitates to lay down spiritual laws. They exist, of course, but who can formulate them? The reader should see in the following lines only a rough sketch of the manner in which God makes saints.

The first thing we can say for certain seems to be this: God is supremely free, and behaves differently with each of his creatures, but from all he requires a profound docility. The sovereign liberty of grace, and in response the fidelity of the soul—this seems to be the primary universal law of holiness. That God is free, that he calls whom he will and in the manner which pleases him, is a basic doctrinal truth. But to any priest who enters the world of souls this truth becomes one of experience. These are the facts which reveal it to him. Supernatural experience teaches him that holiness is not in the first place the product of rules (however necessary they may be), or schedules, or even of states of life, but is the work of grace and of the deep responsiveness of the soul to grace. "See how well I led the Virgin and the saints," Pascal has the Lord saying. Thus it is not a question of trying to outrun grace which has been given to us or of troubling ourselves about what may never be required of us, but of following the grace of each day with the utmost fidelity. Tomorrow may make quite other demands than today; but what matters is today. At this very moment what does grace ask of us? Do it, and we shall receive light for what comes afterwards. It is in this manner that God always leads his saints, and that they allow themselves to be led by him.

The simplicity deriving from love seems to be a second universal law. If God makes saints, always and everywhere he starts from love. And by this word is meant our profound capacity for giving. God deepens, illumines, purifies, expands and utterly regenerates this capacity through his charity. There is not a saint—priest, layman, woman, child—who does not manifest this deepened and widened ability to love, combined with an increase in patience and fortitude. God is constantly teaching them to forget themselves and to love authentically. They may be doing a number of things, but at the center of their lives there is a growth in simplicity. They are caught up in a love which invades their being more and more —and that in the midst of the concrete realities of a life made up of hardship and struggle. This love takes many forms, active and dynamic, silent and hidden, but everywhere—if it comes from God—it is tenacious and always without reserve. It involves renunciation. It leads to "losing one's soul," in the gospel sense—that is, abandoning all self-seeking. Whether it be through our children, through the frustrations of daily life, through conflicts and the burden of anxieties—through all these things God deepens and strengthens his saints' capacity for love. He makes their charity grow in the reality of renunciation.

This genuine supernatural love depends for its development on prayer and silence, and this seems to be a third law of holiness. No doubt the areas of prayer and silence vary widely, according to whether the person concerned is a businessman or a scholar, a housewife or a working woman, a Carmelite or a nursing sister, a monk or the pastor of a densely populated parish. But everywhere the same law of supernatural experience asserts itself: God does not make saints without teaching them to retire to the desert and without moving their hearts. This "desert" takes many forms—an oasis of calm at the steering wheel of one's car; when one is giving a bottle to a baby; during a solitary walk; in the silence of a church; keeping

quite still in the midst of the subway crush—but everywhere
the silence of recollection must be defended and nourished.
Here again a universal law manifests itself: God makes his
saints everywhere, but whatever the circumstances, he asks
for prayer and patiently instructs them in it. We shall not find
anyone, in any milieu whatsoever, who has not in his heart a
little of what might be called a taste for God bestowed by
prayer.

Nor shall we find anyone who has not experienced his own
weakness and whom God has not dealt with like a good vine-
dresser pruning his vine. But it must be noted that our experience of weakness is not always, necessarily salutary. It may
arise from a state of ill health, and we should be in no haste
to glorify it. Illness is not in itself a state of grace. Nevertheless the truth remains that *all* men, in order to come close to
God, must first experience their weakness. For we must learn
to rely not on ourselves but on the immense, all-powerful
grace of God. Whatever form this experience may take, it
leads us to the first Beatitude—Blessed are the poor—which
is the threshold of the kingdom of God. It is accompanied, if
it comes from God, by an increased awareness of his grace.
We are weak indeed; but of far greater consequence is the
fact that God is near and we can fearlessly depend upon him.
It would never strike anyone to call St. Paul a timid man. And
yet he, the Apostle to the Gentiles, declared that if he must
boast he would boast of his weakness: "for God's power is
made perfect in weakness" (2 Co. 12.9). All God's saints have
had this experience, and it is through this that God has made
them saints. God has made all those he has called to intimacy
with him taste the anguish of his Son's cross.

But everywhere he leads them to the victory of hope. Evil

is immense, life is uncertain, the forces of disintegration seem to prevail, and the pagan asks, "Where is your God?" In all the saints, hope has been put to the test, and yet, deep in their hearts, they have all experienced a kind of serenity and even joy, well knowing that God's power is supreme. Resurrection has begun with the crucifixion, and they experience a fore-taste of it. Everywhere they see the risen life springing up. As it did for St. Paul, the risen Christ, the Lord of Glory, lightens their daily horizon. They know that the kingdom of God is coming. Their hope rests on God himself, a hope which transcends the evil of the world. And they stand fast.

These truths are for all ages, and our fathers in the Faith lived them before us. But it may be the privilege of our epoch to see them manifested more clearly than in the past. It may be that in our time a greater outpouring of God's grace is in store for lay people. If so, the only question for us to ask is, "Why, Lord, may your grace not be ours?"

2. Death and Resurrection in Christ

"Do you not know that all of us who have been baptized into Christ Jesus were baptized into his death?" (Rm. 6.3)

Everything in the Christian destiny finds its source in baptism. It is the fountain of living water where the people of God is born. In each of us it is incomparably more than a past event, it is an intimate and permanent reality—namely, it is Christ himself in whom we are immersed. And here, consequently, is the fundamental law of our life and of our holiness: baptized in Christ, we must "put on" Christ; baptized in Christ, we must die daily and rise from the dead with him.

Putting on Christ

Note the expression "baptized into Christ." We were in fact baptized in water; yet this natural element, fluid and vivifying, expresses a much deeper mystery: we are immersed in a living person, we are baptized, and forever. Christian life consists simply and essentially in a mystery of a personal relationship with a Person, with Christ. Let us not see something extraordinary here, something reserved for a few people. It is the very essence of our Christian vocation. Baptized Christians, are you forgetting that, above all things, you were baptized into a divine Person?

How does one meet this Person? Through an act of the

spirit, faith, joined inseparably with an act in which the body
has its part, the sacrament. Not for a moment would St. Paul
or St. John have thought of separating the two, faith and the
sacrament. Had not the Lord said: "Go therefore and make
disciples of all nations, baptizing them" (Mt. 28.19)? Thus,
if the newly baptized wanted to be immersed in water, it was
because he believed in Christ, or, to repeat what Scripture
says, "that Jesus was the Lord." On the other hand, his faith
needed to be expressed in a visible gesture, comprehensible to
all; therefore, he cleansed himself "by the washing of water
with the word" (Ep. 5.26).

Thus he fulfilled the commandment of Jesus and was faithful to the tradition of the newborn Church. His body itself
was brought into contact with the water, with the risen body
of Christ, and his whole self became "a new creation in Christ"
(2 Co. 5.17).

Very early the Christian faith affirmed the fundamental
unity of the creation of God, spirit and matter; the central
place of the risen body of Jesus in the economy of salvation;
and the ecclesial character of Christian life: the neophyte was
baptized in a mystery visibly celebrated by the community.
Faith together with the sacrament was thus affirmed as the
normal way to Christ and to the Church, as it still is in our
day.[1]

At what level is this fundamental union of the baptized with
Christ to be found? On an incomparably deeper level than
that of psychological experience: on the plane of our very

---

[1] Cf. Ga. 3.26–27 where we see how spontaneously St. Paul relates
faith and baptism: "For in Christ Jesus you are all sons of God,
through faith. For as many of you as were baptized into Christ have
put on Christ."

being seized by Christ. It is, of course, normal to see the fruits of this union, and St. Paul describes them. Yet in itself this union is beyond the sphere of consciousness. It is the object of faith, reached only through faith. As St. Paul says, "If anyone is in Christ [baptized], he is a new creation; the old has passed away, behold, the new has come" (2 Co. 5.17). Notice the unique force of the term used—"creation." It was impossible to find a stronger one. It is at this level that our union with Christ is found: on a plane beyond all perception, on a plane which merges with the mystery of our creation itself.

This is the cause of our peace, and often of our suffering as well. Of our peace: for our union with Christ depends neither on our changing moods nor on changing circumstances; it is he himself who has seized us, and nothing save sin can wrest us from his hands. Of our suffering too: for we are by nature beings fashioned for perception, rational spirits ordered towards what seems to be the natural development of things. And God's ways are not our ways, nor is our union with Christ of the order of perceptible experience. All Christian holiness lies in faith, in the deepening of the life of faith, growing constantly in certitude and assimilating our human life to itself more and more, but at the same time deepening also in mystery.

Nevertheless it is constantly the bearer of greater fruit for God. We have noted that St. Paul speaks of fruits of the Spirit which can be experienced even in this life. Tasting them, man knows that God is here. "The fruit of the Spirit is love, joy, peace, patience, kindness, goodness, faithfulness, gentleness, self-control" (Ga. 5.22). All these fruits, tangible yet supernatural, come from the Holy Spirit. At the same time they

derive from our union with Christ. You may perhaps have
noted the way St. Paul expresses this in the quotation cited
above. "Baptized into Christ, you have *put on* Christ" (Ga.
3.27). It is only a figure of speech, of course, but what a
speaking image it is! Putting on Christ means that little by
little Christ takes hold of us in our entirety, converting our
poor human feelings into his own. What is involved is our
forming the habit of constantly turning to him. Here we have
the fundamental law of our baptism and the Christian life.
Instead of a moral principle it is to Christ, living and close
at hand, that we are referred as it were by instinct. It is thus
that we put on Christ or, better still, permit ourselves to be
clothed in him. "Put on the Lord Jesus Christ" (Rm. 13.14),
says St. Paul; and also: "Walk in love, as Christ loved us"
(Ep. 5.2). Everything is said in these few words, and the law
of Christian life and holiness is set down for ever.

Dead and risen with Christ

It is in a very special and decisive way that by entering
into *the mystery of Christ's death and resurrection* our union
with him is brought to authentic realization. Grasp at once
the wonderful realism of this doctrine. Not through our spirit
alone but through our very substance, through our life and
death, we are united to Christ. Christian baptism, far from
easing us out of the great law of suffering and death, incorporates and transfigures it. Here, henceforth, is the road on
which God waits for us and saves us.

And this is so because Christ took this road first. In truth,
God-made-man chose the cross to save us, a cross which, contrary to all human expectation, flowered in the resurrection.

He accepted our world as it was, as a world in which there was suffering and death because of sin. But through his obedience and his life he transformed this fruit of sin into a work of salvation. And whoever follows this same road, in union with him, can believe, in the innermost depths of his soul, that God's life is being made fruitful in him.

Listen again to St. Paul: "Do you not know that all of us who have been baptized into Jesus Christ were baptized into his death?" (Rm. 6.3). Into his death: that is, into his sacred passion, a work of love. And in this passion, what took place? Christ, in the name of us all, died to sin. He rejected in our name, fundamentally, everything that is a refusal of God, everything that involves an obstinate and sinful centering on ourselves. He said yes to God, a yes that was total, absolute, utterly clear. And he said it not only in spirit, in a facile, idealistic way, but with his life, with his suffering, and with his death. This terrible road, which we dread, has become God's road, on which Christ's human will was most closely united to his Father's; on which our will, united to his, finds the way back to paradise.

Thus our baptism effected a fundamental rupture with the world of sin, a cleavage brought about by Christ himself. One who is newly baptized in Christ is in a changed world. No longer does he live in a universe dominated by sin, death and fear. He lives in the world of the Father. Do you realize what this change means? To live in a universe where everything, by natural instinct, is oriented to the Father, to be oneself a man whose entire being has entered into relation with the Father! Such is the new life brought into being at baptism, a life in which everything is oriented to God, "a life to God" (cf. Rm. 6.10).

This new life, this risen life, this life in Christ—all these terms are synonymous—does not come about in a day. It takes a whole life. But we have already laid hold of it in principle, which is the principle of baptism itself: there is no finding oneself in Christ, rising with Christ, unless one has first died in Christ.

This does not mean that we must die to the authentic world of God's creation: the beauty of the earth, our human verities. Christian experience teaches us little by little where the world of sin has entered into the texture of God's creation. That our purgation is so long-drawn-out and often so painful need not astonish us. We have to die to dispositions and attitudes which are too human, too self-centered, in order to be born to the divine outlook, to the dispositions of Christ. Our whole human condition must undergo this transformation in order to be "in Christ." Nothing will subsist in eternal life, in the risen life, except that which has undergone this transformation into Christ.

All this begins with baptism, but only embryonically. To die and rise again with Christ daily, in joy and sorrow, with patience and hope, with faith and love: this constitutes the situation of the baptized Christian and the fundamental law of holiness.

3. Baptized in the Holy Spirit

Christian baptism incorporates us in Christ, but this incorporation in its fullness can be effected only in and by the Holy Spirit. Indeed our life in Christ is a mystery so wholly divine that it can only arise from this divine source. It cannot come from moral effort alone; there must be a new birth. "Truly, truly, I say to you, unless one is born of water and the Spirit, he cannot enter the kingdom of God" (Jn. 3.5). Thus every Christian is "spiritual" by birth, is born of the Spirit; throughout his life he should be guided by his inspiration.

Life in Christ and life in the Spirit

St. Paul uses the expressions "in Christ" and "in the Spirit" almost interchangeably. By so doing he does not mean to imply that Christ and the Holy Spirit are the same Person; it is rather that the action of one cannot be separated from that of the other. Where Christ is, there the Spirit is also, and there is no "life in Christ" except through the Spirit. The Spirit is the sole principle of this divinizing transformation, for each Christian as well as for the body as a whole. Thus we are justified in Christ (Ga. 2.16) or justified by the Spirit (1 Co. 6.11), sanctified in Christ (1 Co. 1.2) or sanctified in the Spirit (Rm. 15.16), sealed in Christ (Ep. 1.13) or sealed in the Holy Spirit (Ep. 4.30). Anyone who knows the force of these expressions in the Pauline writings can be in no doubt that the Holy Spirit holds a central place in St. Paul's thought, as central, indeed, as that of Christ. It could not be otherwise, since the two are inseparable. Again: where Christ is, the Spirit is also, and there can be no "life in Christ" without the Spirit.

Accordingly, the mission of Jesus is presented in St. John and in the Synoptics in this light: it is he who baptizes in the Holy Spirit; this is the work proper to him. John the Baptist exclaims: "I have baptized you with water; but he will baptize you with the Holy Spirit" (Mk. 1.8; cf. Acts 1.5); and: "He on whom you see the Spirit descend and remain, this is he who baptizes with the Holy Spirit" (Jn. 1.33). The regeneration of humanity in the Spirit appears to be the particular mission of the Messiah.

To "baptize in the Holy Spirit"—what does this mean? To baptize, we know, means to immerse; to immerse in water, the fluid, vivifying element which penetrates everywhere, bringing life with it. Now in Holy Scripture it is precisely water which is presented as the symbol of the Holy Spirit (the Breath of God), who permeates the whole of God's creation, giving it life. And this has a special sense in the case of the life of man, formed of the clay of the earth, earthly, into whose nostrils God "breathed the breath of life" (Gn. 2.7). This breath, this exhalation of God himself, means at once the natural human soul (which St. Paul calls *psuké* later on) and a deep relation of similarity between the spirit of man and the spirit of God (*pneuma*). The Jerusalem Bible has a footnote to this effect: "By adopting the term *pneuma*, breath, rather than the term *nous*, spirit, from Greek philosophy, the biblical tradition suggests the profound relationship between the spirit of man and the Spirit of God who impels

and directs it" (Rm. 1.9). Therefore God speaks to man in
the depths of man's soul, and man can hear him. Indeed the
religious history of humanity is constituted precisely by this
ability of man's, either to open his soul to the Spirit of God
or to refuse to do so.

In the fullness of time, Christ came precisely as the one who
baptizes in the Holy Spirit—that is to say, as the one who,
through a unique outpouring of the Spirit as the consequence
of his passion and resurrection, regenerates the human race.
But here the Spirit is revealed as a divine Person: the Holy
Spirit of Love, the Spirit of the risen Lord, and the Spirit of
the Father. It is in him that Christ baptizes, as in living water,
which is at the same time wind and fire. It is in him that, as
the centuries roll on, earthly humanity becomes, little by little,
"spiritual."

In his Second Epistle to the Corinthians (3.7–18) St. Paul
describes the two "economies"—that is, pedagogies—of God;
on the one hand Moses and the Law; on the other the risen
Lord and the Spirit. Nothing in the first is to be held in con-
tempt—we are still living on God's revelation to Moses (Ex.
33.18–23)—but the second, that of the risen Christ and the
Holy Spirit, is incomparably superior. It is new in the absolute
and triumphant sense that the word has in Scripture, and we
are governed by it now. Baptized in Christ and the Holy
Spirit, we live from henceforth in the radiance of the risen
Christ and under the guidance of the Holy Spirit. Have we
grasped the significance of these words? What a breath of air
from great open spaces they bring with them.

Our life in the Spirit

We shall understand our life "in the Spirit" better if we try to set forth several of what might be called notes of authenticity.

1. We shall say in the first place, at the risk of tautology, that it must be a spiritual life—that is, a life animated in its depths by the Holy Spirit. It is quite certain that for St. Paul as well as for St. John, the "life in Christ" is of an entirely different kind from our moral life on the natural level. It is not a question of depreciating the latter but one of distinguishing it from something of a wholly different nature. We must go beyond simple, natural reason and open ourselves to another Spirit, the Spirit of the living God. Listen to the words of the Apostle:

Now we have received not the spirit of the world, but the Spirit by human wisdom but taught by the Spirit. . . . The unspiritual which is from God. . . . And we impart this in words not taught man [left with the sole resources of his nature] does not receive the gifts of the Spirit of God, for they are folly to him, and he is not able to understand them because they are spiritually discerned (1 Co. 2.12–14).

This is the crucial transition, one we cannot make by our natural powers unaided; yet our freedom turns on it. The question here is not of our leading a "moral life" but of our opening ourselves to the spirit and living in communion with him.

2. Our baptismal life is "spiritual"; but moreover it is the life of the sons of God. For the Spirit has no other purpose than to conform us "to the image of his well-beloved Son, in order that he might be the first-born among many brethren"

(Rm. 8.29; cf. Col. 1.15). We all know the great passage in
the Epistle to the Romans in which St. Paul describes our
filial adoption in Christ through the gift of the Spirit. Let us
read it again. Inspired texts must be pondered in silence before
we feel their force.

For all who are led by the Spirit of God are sons of God. For
you did not receive the spirit of slavery to fall back into fear,
but you have received the spirit of sonship. When we cry, "Abba!
Father!" it is the Spirit himself bearing witness with our spirit
that we are children of God, and if children, then heirs, heirs of
God and fellow heirs with Christ [and suddenly this abrupt prob-
ing into our present condition] provided we suffer with him in
order that we may also be glorified with him (Rm. 8.14–17; cf.
Ga. 4.4–7).

Such is the Spirit into which we have been baptized. It
remains for us now to conduct ourselves as sons of God, not
in fear but in freedom, not as commoners but as lords, and
this in the midst of the world's tribulations.

3. It is thus that we shall learn the meaning of Christian
freedom: "for you were called to freedom" (Ga. 5.13). There
is, of course, a false freedom, which gives the "flesh" its opportunity (Ga. 5.13; cf. 1 Pt. 2.16), or leads to a childish assump-
tion of superiority to the law. St. Paul himself teaches that
the law is "holy" and "spiritual" (Rm. 7.12–14), that it is a
pedagogue bringing us to Christ, to find faith (Ga. 3.24).
Nevertheless this same St. Paul fought for Christian freedom.
It must not be forgotten that our salvation in Christ is a new
thing, nor should the gift of the spirit be underestimated.
Henceforth the Christian law is wholly *interior*; it consists in
habitual submission to the Holy Spirit.

In other words, the question we can put to ourselves in this:

wherein resides habitually the power of our conscience to spur us on? Is it in the law, awakening an obscure sense of guilt? Or is it in love and a constantly deepening submission to the Holy Spirit? The fact is that it is here, in love and docility to the Holy Spirit, that the specific power of the Christian conscience to urge us on resides; and it is a power which does not oppress but, on the contrary, liberates us, for "where the Spirit of the Lord is, there is freedom" (2 Co. 3.17).

4. Through this freedom love enters concretely into our lives. Love—charity—flows from the Holy Spirit like water from its source. "God's love has been poured into our hearts through the Holy Spirit which has been given to us" (Rm. 5.5). The law of the Spirit is love, and to live in the Spirit is to live in love; not in some counterfeit that is vague and full of inconsistencies but in a "love that bears all things, believes all things, hopes all things, endures all things" (1 Co. 13.7). The mark of Christian maturity and holiness in Christ's Church is always charity which nothing dismays. There is no better way towards either God or men (1 Co. 12.31). Charity is the bond of perfection, uniting all the virtues (Col. 3.14). What an extraordinary unity and simplicity the Christian life takes on when it is constantly brought back to love and the Holy Spirit!

5. A life in charity—how could life in the Spirit be anything other than ecclesial? The Holy Spirit is constantly invoked by St. Paul as the great life-principle of the Church.

The Holy Spirit forms and animates the body of Christ. "For by one Spirit we were all baptized into one body—Jews or Greeks, slaves or free—and all were made to drink of one Spirit" (1 Co. 12.13). To say "the Holy Spirit" is the same as to say "the Church": both the fundamental unity and the living diversity of services and gifts are the same (1 Co. 12.4–11; cf. Ep. 4.11–13).

An authentic spiritual life cannot but be ecclesial.

6. Both in the Church and in the world, the spiritual life cannot but be a life of apostolic witness. The Church cannot but bear witness to Christ to the uttermost ends of the earth. But who is the great witness of God and of Christ if not the Holy Spirit, whose testimony constitutes the very life of the Church at its center and in all its outward manifestations? "You shall receive power when the Holy Spirit has come upon you; and you shall be my witnesses in Jerusalem and in all Judea and Samaria and to the end of the earth" (Ac. 1.8; cf. Mt. 28.19). The Church of the Holy Spirit cannot but be missionary.

It is impossible for anyone living in the Spirit to be neutral, or simply passive. Is he unmindful of the fact that he has been baptized in the Breath of God which burst forth with violence at Pentecost, and under the form of tongues of fire? No doubt we often feel lost in the midst of a world which gets along without God so easily, and we understand the terrible apprehension in which the prophet lamented: "Ah, Lord God! Behold, I do not know how to speak, for I am only a youth" (Jr. 1.6). St. Paul himself experienced moments of terrible distress (1 Co. 2.3; 2 Co. 1.8). But the Holy Spirit comes to the aid of our weakness with manifestations of force and power (1 Co. 2.4–5). "For God did not give us a spirit of timidity but a spirit of power and love and self-control" (2 Tm. 1.7).

Let us have no fear, then, but speak out boldly, for a great people are in the making for God (Ac. 18.10).

4. Towards the Fullness of Christ

"By one Spirit we were all baptized into one body" (1 Co. 12.13). Do we quite naturally think of our baptism in this light—baptism, the building up of the body of Christ? Let us be done with our narrow outlook and raise ourselves to embrace an immense reality: "You are the body of Christ," St. Paul exclaims (1 Co. 12.27); his body, which is growing unceasingly, until it shall have reached the fullness intended by God's will (Ep. 4.13; Ph. 3.21) in which all are one in him (Ep. 1.10)—Jew and Greek, slave and free, male and female, all things in heaven and on earth (Col. 1.16). Christians, my brothers, what a limitless horizon is opening up before your eyes in your work of each day!

You are a holy people

So far as we can ascertain it in Sacred Scripture, God's design for the world seems to be an endeavor not so much to secure the salvation of the individual as to establish a holy people in whom the destiny of the whole world is contained. It is true, of course, that the gospel teaches us to conduct our personal lives under the gaze of our Father in heaven, thus laying the foundation for the dignity and autonomy of a personal conscience finally answerable to God alone. But there is no conflict between this personal conscience and a collective universal vision, that of the immense body which we together form in Christ. Moreover, our personal conscience is genuinely adult—whether from the divine or the human standpoint—only when it constantly includes in all its workings a vivid awareness of the whole body.

Read, for instance, the biblical account of the calling of Abraham and the promise that his posterity would be more numerous than the stars in heaven (Gn. 15.1–7); the calling of Moses, and God's promise to lead his people out of Egypt (Ex. 3.2–12). Read the allegory of Isaiah's vineyard (5.1–7), which represents "the house of Israel and the men of Juda." Listen to the promises of the prophets concerning the future glory of Jerusalem (Is. 60—62), and you will be convinced that God's design is indeed to form a holy people in whom all the nations of the earth are contained.

With Christ this design was manifested with full clarity. St. John and St. Paul in particular have traced for us the development of this extraordinary showing of God's power and tenderness: the Word was made flesh and dwelt amongst us. In him God became completely God-with-us. In him and through him he forms the holy people which Israel in the desert only prefigured. There is now someone in our midst whom our fleshly eyes cannot see (Jn. 1.26) but whom our faith perceives. There is Christ, ceaselessly growing amongst us. We are his members, we are his body. We are not a collection of separate individuals but one body which is his. Our baptized soul holds in a single embrace Christ, the Holy One, and the myriads of brothers he gives us. The baptismal fonts are not only the place of our personal regeneration but—what tremendous poignancy there is in the thought!—the scene of never ceasing birth and growth in the whole body of Christ.

We know all these things, we even hold them as articles of faith; but how long it takes us to realize their truth in a practical way and bring it to bear on our lives. Take two examples.

To be born to Christ, to transmit to our children not only customs but Christ himself—what a difficult undertaking this sometimes seems. Thus when we are before the crib which we prepare every year, aren't we conscious that our efforts to pass on even the substance of our faith to our children are rather miserable? Have we not difficulty in finding the simple, right words which will convey to them that we really believe in this, we grown-ups? . . . "There is the ox and the donkey; but, more than that, there is God who loved us, there is Christ in our hearts. Let us love one another. Let us love all men, our brothers, and give thanks to God. . . ." It is thus that the body of Christ is built up: through faith in him and through the transmission of this faith in simple and suitable words.

Here is the second example. We had a meeting of our Catholic Action group. Little by little we began to talk to one another, quite simply: we communicated on a deep level in our common faith and in the word of God which we share. We realized, then, that we were a cell in the Church, and that Christ was in the midst of us if we only believed in him and loved one another. And we grasped what was meant by planting the Church and building up the body of Christ. From now on we shall not be content until we have attained this same result at our various Christian meetings. And we shall put our trust in the small grain thus sown and already growing. Baptism, the seed of the body of Christ.

Towards the fullness of Christ

But whither is this immense body of Christ tending? Towards its fullness. The term is St. Paul's. He uses it by preference toward the end of his life, in the epistles which are held to express the fullest development of his thought (Col. 1.19; 2.9; Ep. 4.13). He permits us to share his vision (revealed by God for our instruction) of Christ growing ceaselessly until everything is filled to overflowing. This "fullness" is first of all that of God himself, whose creative presence fills the whole universe (Col. 2.9). But it is also Christ's. First the incarnation (Col. 1.15–19), then the resurrection (1 Co. 15.20–28), and finally the pouring out of the Spirit, have placed Christ, even in his humanity, at the head not only of the race but of the universe.[1] And by "head" is not meant his taking precedence in a remote way. Let us grasp, on the contrary, that this means an intimate, lifegiving presence, hidden and all-powerful, the presence of a Saviour and Lord. This presence is extended over the whole of humanity; and in humanity, it is extended first of all over the body of the baptized, who are the leaven of the whole. Then, as a consequence, it will be extended to the whole universe, caught up in our salvation as it was in our fall. (Read, in this connection, the extraordinary passages in Romans, 8.19–22, and Philippians, 3.21.)

Thus, before all things there is Christ, the Living, the First and the Last, the First-born from the dead (Rev. 1.17; Col. 1.18). Then there is the body of the baptized, plunged into his death and his resurrection. But the Holy Spirit is free. He seeks out whom he will (Ac. 10.47) and makes him a member of Christ—that is, if in his heart he consents.

[1] See the note on Col. 1.19 in the Jerusalem Bible.

There are not two Churches, a visible Church made up of the baptized and an invisible Church made up of men of good will visited by the Holy Spirit. There is but one Church, one body of Christ, made up of the baptized become one with Christ, the leaven of the whole world.

The Church of Christ has never known any way but one of contributing to the growth of the body of Christ: to preach the word, to pour the water of the sacraments, to show forth her unity and holiness to men. All this is in some sense visible; this is what Christ willed and commanded. But this visible Church he desired to be a sign and a standard lifted up among the nations, so that through her the true God should be known. And while she remains the holy Church of Christ, she must enter more and more into dialogue with the world which God wills to save and to bring into unity in his Son. Thus it is not towards the past but towards the future that her course is directed, in order to bring into being the perfect Man, according to "the measure and the stature of the fullness of Christ" (Ep. 4.13).

Everything is possible to God

Have you noted the force of supernatural optimism contained in the 1962 Christmas message of John XXIII? He takes it upon himself to make contact with all men of good will of our times, with those who are sincerely in search of peace, with manual workers as well as scientists, with fathers and mothers and their children. Along with the Council Fathers he exults with hope, stressing the powerful movement towards unity stirring among Christians and through the whole world. Would not St. Paul have exulted too, and discerned, through the signs of our times, the coming of Christ, and his body growing towards the fullness planned by God?

When we see so many hard faces, so many evidences of sin in the world, doubtless we may ask ourselves, Is it possible that God should will to love men—these men we are looking at—to the point of making up of them the body of his Son?

And yet this is all the teaching of our faith, that which Jesus declared in obscure terms and St. Paul proclaimed throughout the known world of his time. Let us dare to believe it and an immense hope will take hold of us. No, our old humanity is not drifting towards one knows not what— the superman of the future, a prospect tempting and terrifying at the same time. Slowly, through its struggles and discords, its joys and trials, its faith and love, it is becoming each day a little more the holy dwelling of God and the body of his Son.

5. Live for God

It is above all towards God, towards the contemplation of his glory, that baptism orients us. Surely you remember the triumphant words of St. Paul which the Church has us sing on Easter Day: "For we know that Christ being raised from the dead will never die again; death no longer has dominion over him. The death he died he died to sin, once for all, but the life he lives he lives to God" (Rm. 6.9–10). The original text is very nearly untranslatable. It might be paraphrased as follows: "All that which lives in him lives to God." Let us weigh these words: a life in which everything soars up towards God and lives for him! Such is the life of the risen Christ. Such is our life, to the extent that we are risen with him. Fundamentally, it is a life-to-God which baptism initiates in us and tends to develop. Baptism, seed of contemplation; baptism, seed of glory!

St. Ignatius of Antioch, in chains and on the way to his martyrdom, wrote to the Christians of Rome: "I have within me a living water, murmuring, and saying to me, inwardly, 'Come to the Father.'"[1] This living water is the water of our baptism. In the uproar of the cities, in the midst of our sorrows as well as our joys, it whispers to us, interiorly: "God is, and he is here, very near us."

[1] *Epître aux Romains*, VII, 2. In *Les Ecrits des Pères apostoliques* (Coll. "Chrétiens de tous le temps," No. 1), p. 175.

The life of our baptism is thus deeply *theologal*. By this we are to understand not only that it is superterrestrial in its origin, comes from God, but still more that it is directed towards him. Through it we are ordered to him, above all else, as an object. When St. Thomas is speaking of man's direct relation with God, he always specifies its term by the same word: *Ipse*, God himself. The life of the Christian is bound up with the work of the world, and we do not give glory to God if our contemporaries do not feel that we are deeply committed to the struggles in which they are hard pressed. Nevertheless our baptism does not order us primarily towards earthly concerns. It carries us upward and inward. It directs us towards God himself, God in person: God, Christ, to whom the heart of the baptized Christian cries out, to whom it responds with love. Our life is first of all a life of personal relationship with God.

That is why we have, deep in our souls, "eyes made to see him." Our Lord teaches us: "Blessed are the pure in heart, for they shall see God" (Mt. 5.8). And St. John, the disciple he loved, becomes his faithful echo: "When he appears we shall be like him, for we shall see him as he is" (1 Jn. 3.2). These words—"they shall see God," "we shall see him as he is"—have come down the centuries. They carry an immeasurable hope with them: Some day we shall see him. And already, in this life, we can converse with him in faith.

There is no remote suggestion in this of a spiritual luxury reserved to a few initiates. It is the fundamental condition of the baptized, our "blessed" condition. Above all, it is at this level that our baptism causes us to live.

St. Paul describes this condition particularly by talking constantly about *glory*: our baptism is glorious. Already in this life, in the midst of death, the glory of Christ comes upon us. We know that in the Old Testament this term glory—the glory of Yahweh—was reserved to God. Moses asked: "I pray thee, show me thy glory" (Ex. 33.18). And God answered: "You cannot see my face, for man shall not see me and live." But when the Son came, full of grace and truth, "we beheld his glory" (Jn. 1.14). Thenceforth the light of his glory shines in the souls of the baptized. Let us ponder these extraordinary words: "And we all, with unveiled face, beholding the glory of the Lord, are being changed into his likeness from one degree of glory to another" (2 Co. 3.18).

And let us not cry out that we are parting with earth. The amazing thing about Christian revelation is precisely that through it heaven and earth—or, in other words, suffering and glory—are so strongly united. Moreover, this word "suffering," dear to St. Paul, expresses a permanent aspect of the human condition, particularly where the apostle is concerned. On this earth we are in the midst of suffering; yet, at the same moment, we are in glory. Hence for St. Paul, in the thick of his sufferings, joy abounds (Col. 1.24). He is not talking thoughtlessly here; he knows from experience what hunger, thirst, nakedness and persecution are. And yet he exclaims: "For this slight momentary affliction is preparing for us an eternal weight of glory beyond all comparison" (2 Co. 4.17).

Note this well: in speaking of glory here, St. Paul is not simply playing with words. For him it is already as much a reality as the grievous sufferings he calls slight. He is not talking about nebulous things but about actual realities. Baptism is truly a weight of glory. "And we await a Saviour, the Lord Jesus Christ, who will change our lowly body to be like his glorious body" (Ph. 3.20–21).

It should, then, be our normal condition to be full of exulta-
tion, of joy, of thanksgiving and praise to the glory of God.
Our baptism makes us, above all, men who give glory to God,
and this even in our death: "This he [Jesus] said to show by
what death he was to glorify God" (Jn. 21.19). Reread certain psalms,[2] certain canticles[3] in the Bible, the epistles of the
Apostles;[4] listen in your heart to the words of the *Gloria in
excelsis Deo* or those of our marvellous *Te Deum*, and you
will see that our religion is above all a religion of God; above
all, it makes us glorify God.

Live to the world

But let us not set in opposition things which God has
united. It is not a question of God on one side and man on
the other; on the one hand a religion centering on the glory
of God and on the other a religion centering on the salvation
of man. There is but one Lord, the only Son of the Father,
sharing with him the one same glory, who for us and for our
salvation became incarnate in the womb of a virgin. Our
baptism places us in a living relationship with God, but at the
same time it places us in a living relationship with our brothers;
it orients us towards God in Person, and it orients us also
towards the world, which is to be consecrated to God.

For the world does not, unhappily, live for God, and yet
it is fundamentally God's world. It is likewise Christ's world,

---

[2] Especially psalms 95, 96, 97, 98, 99, 102, 135, etc.

[3] Cf., for example, the eighteen biblical canticles in the psalter of
the Jerusalem Bible.

[4] Among others, Rm. 11.33–36; 1 Co. 15.54–58; Ep. 1.3–14; 3.14–21;
Ph. 2.6–11; Col. 1–15, 20; 3.12–17; 1 Tm. 3.16; 6.15–16, etc.

"for in him all things were created" (Col. 1.16; Jn. 1.3). Our
task as baptized Christians, then, is to play a part in leading
the world to God. To this end, we must first *see* it as coming
from him and returning to him: "O Lord, our Lord, how
majestic is thy name in all the earth!" (Ps. 8.1); "The sea is
his for he made it; for his hands formed the dry land" (Ps.
95.5). In particular we must train ourselves to see man, our
brother, as reflecting on his countenance the Face of God
(Ps. 4.6); and not man in the abstract but man in the concrete, the only one who exists—the man with whom we work,
live, cooperate. He is baptized, or baptizable. He is the bearer
of a treasure whose existence, owing to appearances which
are deceptive, irritating or even repulsive, may not always be
suspected. He bears a likeness to God, even if it is buried or
disfigured. He is capable, even as we are, of suffering and
love. Like us, he will die and appear before God. Like us, he
is a mystery which God alone can fathom. If we cannot talk
to him, we can at least pray and love him in silence. In this
way we can bring him into relation with the heavenly Father
and help to spread over him the radiance of the divine glory
and love.

But it is not enough to *see* them, man and the world, in the
light of God. We must unite ourselves to them in the sense of
accepting them, as they are, into the embrace of our love. It
is thus that Christ has saved us: by embracing us and uniting
us to himself. The mystery of his union with humanity is
extolled in Scripture in terms of an espousal. And as for us:
following Christ and with him, we can be his saving instruments only through those things which we have espoused
and to which we unite ourselves daily: this task, this profession, this labor. A deep seriousness, great loyalty, much com-

petence will be required of us, and great joy. The grace we have as baptized Christians can draw the world to God only under this condition.

Here we shall also find the cross. We shall soon discover that the cross does not come from the outside but is built into our life—that is, to return to the terms of our discussion, into those very things which we have espoused: our home, profession, responsibilities; our idealism; the work of the Church; and so on. There, too, Christ enlightens us: it is on the cross that he united himself to us, on the cross that he saved us. His cross saves, for it is his unfeigned love. In the same way our miseries make it possible to give to God and to our brothers a love with no falseness in it. And therefore with Christ and in him, the glory of the resurrection already shines upon them.

At other moments there is great joy, human and divine, and it is a wonder to us: "Praise the Lord from the heavens . . . praise him from the earth . . . young men and maidens together, old men and children!" (Ps. 148). "Bless the Lord, O my soul, and forget not all his benefits" (Ps. 103.1–2).

God alone is holy

If the world reconciled with God is already so beautiful, what must be the beauty of God himself? A whole current of Christian tradition is so overwhelmingly conscious of this transcendent difference between God and ourselves that without in any way denying the goodness of the world, it is unable to take its eyes off God. St. Bruno falls to his knees and exclaims: "O *Bonitas*! O divine Goodness!" Such is the testimony of the contemplatives. They remind us that if the world is beautiful, God is incomparably more lovely still. They make manifest the most fundamental vocation of our baptism: You must be "alive to God" (Rm. 6.11).

Here on earth it is normal that there should be a tension between the two vocations inherent in our baptism which is painful yet fruitful: being alive to God and alive to the world. Sometimes this can be a torment to us. May God grant that this torment shall be suffered under the influence of his authentic charity. But also, in the normal course of events, God confers on us, little by little, a share in his own integrity. And then we shall know how to glorify him as the only Holy One and how to work for our brothers. Baptism: the seed of contemplation and of glory, in heaven and on earth.

6. To Fulfill Man

The grace of baptism transcends all earthly things, rising to God himself: Be "alive to God," St. Paul tells us (Rm. 6.11). But at the same time this grace also makes us more human. More specifically, it fulfills man insofar as it perfects and purifies him on the level of his human nature. If St. Paul could reproach the pagans for being "heartless" and "ruthless" (Rm. 1.31), the grace of baptism, by contrast, breaks the "heart of stone" in us and gradually develops the "heart of flesh" (Ez. 11.19) which renders us more sensitively aware of God and our brothers. And perhaps these are the two things our unbelieving brothers ask of us most imperatively: "Live your life for God," they say, "and show us through your life a God who is God." On the other hand they ask us to be men, real men, passionately committed, along with them, to all human affairs.

He knew what is in man

The question is not a simple one, for in man's nature there are tares among the good wheat. Clearly we shall find in Holy Scripture no trace of facile humanism or easy optimism. God saw in the beginning that everything in his creation was good (Gn. 1.10); but how solemn Jesus' words are when he refers

37

to man. St. John says: "Jesus did not trust himself to them, because he knew all men and needed no one to bear witness of man; for he himself knew what was in man" (Jn. 2.24–25). How he has plumbed the depths of our hearts! He knew what was in man. . . .

We shall see later that, although he knew men, he did not despair of us. Let us for the moment, however, stress the seriousness and even severity of tone which God adopts in speaking to man, whether through the prophets or through the Son of his love: "O men, how long will you love vain words, and seek after lies" (Ps. 4.2); "O faithless generation, how long am I to be with you? How long am I to bear with you?" (Mk. 9.19). The prophet knew that man is like "grass that withers, flowers that fade" (Is. 40.7), or like the "dust" scattered by the wind, or like the fragile "flesh"; Christ, who knew all this and infinitely more, said repeatedly to his disciples: "Watch and pray that you may not enter into temptation; the spirit indeed is willing, but the flesh is weak" (Mt. 26.41). The psalmist knew that "men are all a vain hope" (Ps. 116.11), and the disciple whose vocation it was to believe in Love (1 Jn. 4.16) writes: "If we say we have no sin, we deceive ourselves, and the truth is not in us" (1 Jn. 1.8). St. Paul, who more than any other has exalted the sovereign freedom of man in Christ, speaks most somberly, almost tragically, of the terrible aberrations of man left to himself, "boastful inventors of evil . . . foolish, faithless, heartless, ruthless" (Rm. 1.30–31). These few reminders are enough to show us the extraordinarily grave view which Christ takes of our condition. Yes, he knew—as no moralist will ever know—what is in man.

And yet he did not despair of us. He trusted himself to our hands. He trusted us, confiding in his grace at work in us and in the sound spiritual foundations laid by his Father and himself, with the Holy Spirit, from our first days on earth.

And God saw that all this was good

For it is in one same movement that creation and redeeming grace brought us forth from the earth. When he formed man of dust from the ground (Gn. 2.7), God knew about his fall —our countless falls—but he was also thinking of his Son who would be born of a virgin. And he made our flesh good. The Evil One might come, but he would not corrupt the whole. Man would be healed, renewed, he would not be destroyed. God, if we may put it that way, would use the same materials: man would remain man. Christ's grace would perfect him from within. He would always be a true man formed of the dust of the earth, but refashioned according to the image of him who was to come, and finally transformed in him.[1]

Therefore, "when the time had fully come, God sent forth his Son, born of woman, born under the law . . . so that we might receive adoption as sons" (Ga. 4.4–5). We know that his being man was no pretense; he was truly man. He did not reject our human happiness; he had a mother and a home. He

[1] Theology has little by little clarified the delicate questions of the relations between nature and grace and the extent of the wounds inflicted on nature by sin. St. Thomas holds that even after sin human nature retains three main features: the thirst for happiness that no limited good can quench, which is the root of freedom; the orientation to truth; and an inclination to the reasonable good. But we lack balance in virtue. In the order of the good we are, without grace, half paralyzed, and our choices are deflected to partial goods. (*Summa Theologica*, I–II, q. 108)

was not without heart, without pity; he had friends, he could weep. He did not despair of man; he confided in his apostles, simple and straightforward men, though full of defects. He gave them the keys of his kingdom. He entrusted them with what he loved most: his mother and his Church. He saw into the heart of Peter and knew that it was true; that Peter loved him. He entrusted him with his sheep (Jn. 21.15–17).

If he, the Lamb of God who takes away the sin of the world, came back on earth, concealing his divine nature as he did before, he would recognize, side by side with the incredible sin of men, the good things his Father made. His glance would penetrate deeper than ours into our misery, but at the same time he would awaken the truest instincts of our hearts: the sound foundation his Father laid, on which his grace builds. He would be more perceptive than we are with regard to the foundation for grace present even in our contemporary world. He would, perhaps, approve of the straight furrows, the loyal and open hands, the candid looks, the friendship among men, the growing sense of solidarity and of social justice, the anger roused by the intolerable scandal of the hungry. It is certain that he would denounce the dreadful evils, particularly those brought about by money and power—"heartless and ruthless" (Rm. 1.31). Surely he would flog other pharisaisms far subtler and more cynical than those of his time. But he would also without doubt recognize a multitude of humble people and upright men from whose midst he would raise up his apostles: "I thank thee, Father, Lord of heaven and earth, that thou hast hidden these things from the wise and understanding and revealed them to babes" (Mt. 11.25).

Our baptism, by plunging us into the life of this same perfect Christ-Man, tends to render us more deeply human, to bring us close to all men, enabling us to engage them in lifelong dialogue.

Whatever is true

Have you noticed this long sentence in St. Paul's Epistle to the Philippians (4.8–9)? Read it slowly, weighing every word. It could be called the program of Christian humanism: "Brethren, whatever is true, whatever is honorable, whatever is just, whatever is pure, whatever is lovely, whatever is gracious, if there is any excellence, if there is anything worthy of praise, think about these things." Gather up from the world all that is true, noble; all these things belong to us, must fill our minds. Nothing of this is foreign to God. Do we understand the full implications of this?

The same St. Paul—whose supremely God-centered attitude is surely unquestionable—is the one who gives to the sublime love of charity—so sublime that it is not of earthly origin but comes from God alone—a humble human aspect: "Love is patient and kind; love is not jealous or boastful; it is not arrogant or rude [the famous discretion or prudence so dear to the ancients]. Love does not insist on its own way; it is not irritable or resentful; it does not rejoice at wrong, but rejoices in the right. Love bears all things, believes all things, hopes all things, endures all things" (1 Co. 13.4–7).

Thus the fruits of the Spirit mentioned by the Apostle are at once deeply human and of divine origin. Here again let us pause: "love, joy, peace, patience, kindness, goodness, faithfulness, gentleness, self-control" (Ga. 5.22–23); note "faithfulness . . . self-control"—such are the fruits of the Holy

Spirit growing in human soil. How much human truth and beauty there is in them!

Again, the same St. Paul: "And it is my prayer that your love may abound more and more, with knowledge and all discernment, so that you may approve what is excellent, and may be pure and blameless for the day of Christ" (Ph. 1.9–10). There is, then, in the baptized a refined discernment based on love. The baptized Christian may lack sophistication, humanly speaking, and yet be delicately perceptive in both a supernatural and human way.

Often poor people have a sensitivity lacking in the rich. The intelligence of simple, straightforward people is frequently surprising. The grace of baptism enables us to become like this, deeply compassionate and perceptive, aware of things which others do not see—for instance, the hidden dignity of the humiliated and the ridiculed. May God grant that we, the baptized, shall give to the world the testimony of such men, who are fashioned after Christ.

They glorify your Father

Sometimes holiness is presented in terms of such perfection —or rather, in terms of such unreality—that the man can no longer be recognized in the saint. Such "saints" have lost their human personality. The tares have been uprooted with so much haste that much of the surrounding soil has come with them, and the good wheat as well. This is the famous "purity in a vacuum" of which Mounier spoke. Let us not rush in with our disclaimers; those days are not over yet. Too many Christians, men and women, seem lacking in human vitality. It is not through any fault in their baptism; rather, it is due to an education which emphasizes the negative and is based on fear; yet, at the same time, is satisfied with itself. Or perhaps these Christians have an ideal of perfection too exclusively restricted to the individual or the family. Their own clear consciences and the respectability of their family are their moral preoccupations, to the exclusion of almost all else. This is good, of course, but it is not enough. They lack human substance. Disciples of God-made-man, they lack interest in their fellow men and any real love for them.

Our contemporaries make terrible demands of us in this respect. They insist, almost violently, that we must be men as they are, only more so. It is not a matter of forgetting God. Alas, we forget him far too often. In the midst of a world which seems to be drifting further and further into a practical materialism, what is demanded of us is that we bear witness to God with our whole being, to a holy and personal God, one who alone is good and holy. "Live to God!" St. Paul keeps exclaiming. But this God loves man to the point of having restored him in his most intimate depths by himself becoming man. If we learn to look at Christ the way the grace of our baptism teaches us to look at him—with faith and love —we shall learn truly to be men. We shall then understand and love the men of our time, *one of whom we are*. And perhaps, seeing us, "they will glorify the Father who is in heaven" and will dare to believe that infinitely above man, and yet loving him, there is God.

7. The Christian Contest

We know the great scene which "opens"[1] the public life of our Lord, as well as of his Church; Jesus was led into the desert to engage in his first, and decisive, contest with the Evil One. At the end of his life he underwent another contest, more terrible still, that of his agony[2] (Mk. 14.32–42). His public life is bounded by these two contests. They do not end in defeat and death but in victory and the glory of God. "To him who conquers I will grant to eat of the tree of life which is in the paradise of God" (Rev. 2.7). And his reign will never end.

He was led into the wilderness to be tempted by the devil

The desert holds a central place in the history of the people of God and of any soul in search of God. The Lord led forth his people to the desert "and guided them in the wilderness like a flock" (Ps. 78.52). In the desert the soul is purified, disencumbered, brought back to essentials. In the desert took place Israel's first meeting with the love of God, and despite her weaknesses she remained faithful to him. Later, in contact

[1] In the sense of an overture, as to an opera, giving the essential theme.

[2] Agony, from the Greek *agon*, means contest, final contest.

with the nations of the world and an easier way of life, she did not resist compromises; she exchanged "the incorruptible glory of God" for idols. Therefore God had to bring Israel back to the desert often in order to reach her heart.[3]

Thus the desert is, above all, a place of meeting with God. Whoever wants to find God must accept the desert as an inescapable part of his life. Our Lord gives us this great lesson: before entering into the contest for which he had been sent into the world, he retired to the desert, where he fasted and prayed. It is the same for us; we cannot carry on our Christian combat if we do not retire with Christ into solitude and pray and fast with him.

The desert is indwelt, first of all, by God, but the Lord allows the Adversary[4] to show himself here, in order to test and strengthen his servants. From this comes the terse, forceful statement of St. Matthew: "Then Jesus was led up by the Spirit into the wilderness to be tempted by the devil" (Mt. 4.1). God permitted this face-to-face encounter so that we might understand what the struggle involved and through what weapons the Messiah emerged the victor: through a serene and heroic fidelity to the Word.

There is this further consequence of the law: we must accept the desert in order to find God, but we shall be probed and tested in it. For we must first experience our radical

[3] On the desert theme, cf. Hos. 2.14; Is. 40.3–5; Jr. 2.2–3. To bring Israel back to God a more terrible desert than that of the Exodus will be required, the desert of exile and captivity.

[4] The Adversary is the Hebrew name for the Evil One; in Greek he is the Devil or the Slanderer. He is the adversary of God's design for humanity, the adversary of Christ, the adversary of Christians. In this dreadful combat (Ep. 6.10) the Christian is united to Christ by faith and by prayer (Mt. 6.13; 26.41) and is the victor (Rev. 12.7–11).

poverty in order to discover the true source of our strength: prayer, and the faith in God which begins with fear and trembling. But it is at this very moment that the Adversary enters the game, perhaps when we are tired and disgusted. "He found them sleeping for sorrow" (Luke 22.45–46), St. Luke says of the three apostles Christ loved most dearly in the garden of the agony. But we hear the word, too, which disperses the darkness: "Why do you sleep? Rise and pray that you may not enter into temptation." It is this dread threshold of temptation that we must refuse to cross, at whatever cost. Listen to St. Paul:

And to keep me from being too elated by the abundance of revelations, a thorn was given me in the flesh, a messenger of Satan, to harass me, to keep me from being too elated. Three times I besought the Lord about this, that it should leave me; but he said to me, "My grace is sufficient for you, for my power is made perfect in weakness" (2 Co. 12.7–9).

It is with these weapons that Christ fought: the weakness of his human nature—"He was hungry" (Lk. 4.2); the word of God, to which he was bound above all things—"You shall worship the Lord your God" (Lk. 4.8; Mt. 4.10).

Having exhausted all temptation

St. Luke uses this word "exhausted" advisedly (Lk. 4.13). Doubtless we must not understand it too literally. And yet the three temptations of Christ in the desert do seem to "exhaust" the temptations which can assail the people of God and the man of faith to put them off course, deflect them from the way God has ordained. "Command these stones to become loaves of bread" (Mt. 4.3). Obviously we all have an absolute need for material bread, and if we do not struggle for this bread of humanity our contemporaries will have a right to challenge our witness. Christian combat does not empty human combat of its substance. And yet the question does not reduce itself to one of human struggle alone. If we are not really hungry for something other than earthly bread, we are not yet full of the Spirit of Christ and we are unfit for his combat. One way or another, we shall turn aside from his path.

"Throw yourself down; for it is written, 'He will give his angels charge of you,' and 'On their hands they will bear you up'" (Mt. 4.5–7). Here we see the temptation of a way of life which presents itself as Christian but which does not pass through the realities of the human situation; unconsciously it asks for signs and wonders, dreaming of a God made to satisfy our whims or of a God put at our disposal by our rites, our rectitude and our good conscience. Holiness does not take this route; it is attained in the context of ordinary life, in which one learns to do God's will and to abandon oneself to his completely free and sovereign grace: "You shall not tempt the Lord your God" (Mt. 4.7).

"To you I will give all this authority and their glory [that of the kingdoms of the earth]" (Lk. 4.5–7). The temptation of political power: to promote the kingdom of God through the force of the secular arm. The history of the Church demonstrates well enough the terrible reality of this temptation, one which assails us all at one time or another. We distrust Christ's weapons, which are love and the cross, and take up the arms of our adversaries: power and influence, wholly detached from love and the cross.

Put on the armor of God

In order to engage in our combat, human and Christian, we have an absolute need of weapons. It would be folly to set out unarmed. Listen to the old warrior, Paul, Apostle of Christ, when he cries to us: "Put on the armor of God" (Ep. 6.11–17).

We must first divest ourselves of one illusion: the idea that we do not have to fight—or anyway not as much as the Church says—or that our battle is over. A formidable illusion, this, for at the very moment when we lay down our arms we are taken by surprise and conquered, if only by sleep overwhelming us in the middle of life. What a lovely triumph for the Adversary! He holds sway over people who are asleep. In view of this the urgency, even the anguish, of our Lord's words becomes understandable: "Why do you sleep? Rise and pray that you may not enter into temptation" (Lk. 22.46). If you are asleep, you are conquered already.[5]

We must put on our armor. But what is it? "Put on the Lord Jesus Christ," says St. Paul (Rm. 13.14). First of all, our armor is a Person. It is wholly interior, wholly living. It is Christ with his Holy Spirit, Christ of the Beatitudes, Christ terrible to the demons, the sinless Christ; Christ of the Cross and Christ of Easter: "Christ, be under me! Christ, be over me! Christ, be beside me, on left hand and right!" sang St. Patrick.

St. Paul has been at pains to describe our weapons in detail.[6]

---

[5] It is the whole sober theme of evangelical vigilance. In the night of this world we must be like watchmen.

[6] Cf. Ep. 6.10.17; 1 Th. 5.4–9; 2 Co. 6.7–8.

It would be folly to advance into the midst of the world with our chest exposed; hence there is the shield of faith. Yes, to put on faith, to armor ourselves with faith—that is our shield. With this, we are ready for battle. "I have kept the faith," said St. Paul shortly before his death (2 Tm. 4.6–7); and St. John said: "This is the victory that overcomes the world, our faith" (1 Jn. 5.4–5).

But we must also have a helmet. Here is where hope comes in (Ep. 6.17; 1 Th. 5.8). In our struggle we must be able to see ahead of us, to tend towards the future, towards Christ, whose advent is for ever. Let us set out; the road down the centuries lies open.

We need a sword, too. Here it is: the word of God. Don't be afraid, speak out boldly.

You must be swift and sure-footed; so, be shod with zeal for propagating the gospel of peace (Is. 52.7; Ep. 6.15). A breastplate? Take faith again (Ep. 6.15). And above all, charity—love. With faith, it is your shield. Arm yourself with love (1 Th. 5.8). Now you can go forth into the midst of the world; you will keep the Spirit of Christ.

Baptism gives us these weapons of the sons of light (1 Th. 5.4–9). We must use them throughout our life, "in honor and dishonor . . . in afflictions, hardships, calamities . . . by forbearance, genuine love, and the power of God" (cf. 2 Co. 6.4–10). Have we noticed how often our Lord says to us, in the gospels, "Do not fear"? With Christ we can conquer fear, and when fear is overcome, we can undertake every-thing. "In the world you have tribulation; but be of good cheer, I have overcome the world" (Jn. 16.33).

8. I Press on Towards the Goal

You know the words of St. Paul—ardent, urgent—when he is describing his race toward Christ: "Not that I have already obtained this . . . but I press on to make it my own, because Christ Jesus has made me his own. Brethren, I do not consider that I have made it my own; but one thing I do, forgetting what lies behind and straining forward to what lies ahead, I press on toward the goal" (Ph. 3.12–14). Oh, the man we see through these lines! Just such a man should the baptized Christian be. Caught up by Christ, he should never pause on his course but with increasing determination should press on towards the goal.

Let yourselves be seized by Christ

Now as human experience testifies, a variety of things conspire to slow us down on our course towards Christ: worldly preoccupations, disappointments, the wear and tear of life, fatigue. Can we keep on running?

And yet—the wonder of it!—we receive at baptism a life which soars up towards God without falling back and—the direct opposite of human life—should never be *on the wane.* Here we have a marvellous thing: God calls us, Christ has laid hold of us, and we shall be held ever more closely if we remain faithful. There is a dynamism here which is inexhaustible; there are "second calls" at a deeper level, more decisive, than the first.

What is the reason for this? The presence of Christ; he has laid hold of us. He has taken, as always, the initiative. How deep this happiness is! We are acquainted, perhaps, with the dictum of Father Peyriguère, the disciple of Father de Foucauld: "Let yourselves be seized by Christ."[1] He always brought his correspondents back to this great objective reality. Why run as if we were the only ones concerned, as if everything depended on our resolution and the strength of our will? If Christ does not take hold of us, we run in vain; we become breathless and are soon overcome by time. But, thank God, there is Christ, and he is the wellspring of our freedom. It is a matter of letting ourselves be grasped by him each day, since this is what he wants; the "yes" we say to him should constantly come from a deeper level of our being. Here is the only source of holiness. But it is real.

Can one try to define psychologically the way in which he takes hold of us? In the final analysis it is through the attraction of his person and the appeal which his kingdom makes to our idealism. The whole dynamism of the Church can be traced back to this twofold source.

First of all, there is his person. All the saints have their eyes fixed on Christ; the whole Church is ceaselessly re-forming itself into the likeness of its Lord. There is no doubt that the knowledge of Christ has a complete history. Grounded in the beginning in ordinary perception, it grows increasingly more mysterious. "Even though we once regarded Christ from a human point of view, we regard him thus no longer," St. Paul

---

[1] *Ecrits spirituels*: "Laissez-vous saisir par le Christ" (Paris, Centurion, 1963).

says (2 Co. 5.16). Christ dwells, like his Father, "in unap-
proachable light" (1 Tm. 6.16). He is the Holy One of God,
the Son of the eternal Father. "It is to your advantage that I
go away" (Jn. 16.7). In the last analysis it means a gain in
our knowledge of him when we cling to him as he is hidden
in the mystery of his glory, unrecognizable to the eyes of the
flesh. It does not matter whether he has shown us his face;
men like ourselves have known him, lived with him, loved
him. His example, his presence, his grace—all these things are
brought to bear on us. But in order to see him, we must learn
to pause and gaze on him often in faith. Only then does he
grasp us, instruct us, convert us.

With Christ, and inseparable from him, are his saints. Their
attraction, their example, disturbs us and prods us on our way.
There are the canonized saints—Francis, Dominic, Bernadette,
Thérèse, to mention only a few. There are the earthly "saints"
of our acquaintance: this chronic invalid whom we never
hear complaining; this mother of a family carrying burdens
to the limit of her endurance; this layman working tirelessly
in face of immense obstacles; that laywoman consecrated to
God in the midst of the world. These people are not the
projection of impossible ideals. They are living, and at an even
deeper level than the rest of us. Their example, the holiness
of their lives, are like a contagion. They set us on our way.
Through them, too, Christ takes hold of us.

He also grasps us through the calls which come to us from
his Church and from the world of men. There is no danger
here that we shall turn inward on ourselves in an unconsciously egotistical search for our own perfection. The needs
are real, serious, urgent: more social justice, a more human
education for the rising generation, the preaching of Christ to

thousands of children without a Christian family, the care of
multitudes of the sick and of abandoned old people. Obviously
we cannot do everything, and we soon reach the limit of our
resources. But with the help of God we have an obligation
to do something, however humble it may appear, and to do
it seriously. In other words, we may not remain dilletantes
and triflers; we must commit ourselves. History bears witness
that this marks the true beginning of our progress towards
God. May we never pause.

Sell what you possess

In order to run faster we must not let ourselves be weighed
down. Hence our Lord's injunction: "Go, sell what you have"
(Mk. 10.21).

Here we are concerned with the counsels of the Lord,
which, as we know, can be efficaciously grasped only within
the context of a living charity. Let us sum up our memory of
the doctrine. The precepts lay down the essential directions
for charity; the counsels propose the ways which of themselves, more swiftly and surely, lead to the perfection of charity. It must be clear to us, however, that the counsels are not
distinct from the precept par excellence, that of charity; they
are of its essence and relate to those gifts of the Spirit infused
into the souls of all the baptized.

We shall grasp this doctrine more fully if by counsels we
understand the secret calls of charity. The fact is that charity
is not summed up in any written law; on the contrary, it is a
living law whose determining characteristic is that of having
no limits: "You shall love the Lord with all your heart and
all your strength." Now, in calling for unlimited growth,

charity involves another demand, the demand for detachment amounting to the total stripping of oneself, which is the concrete condition and the normal effect of the growth of charity. Our Lord in the gospel formulates the general call to self-renunciation and shows the limits to which it may go when he says: "Sell what you have." And he says this to everyone, and all are committed to it. But he leaves it up to each individual to decide specifically what he should sell and how he should sell it.

In other words, the Lord's counsels are calls inherent in the very life of charity. Christ himself put them into words in certain of his utterances (for instance, the episode of the rich young man, Mk. 10.17–22); even more, he demonstrated them by example. They indicate the general direction to be taken —to sell what one has in order to grow in charity—but he leaves it to the prudence of each individual to decide in concrete detail what his course shall be.[2] Thus it is up to each of us to search his own heart in all sincerity, weigh his personal situation—health, abilities, various responsibilities—and decide freely the manner in which he will follow the Lord's counsels.

The religious life consists in a following of these counsels which involves their total and effective realization: for love of our Lord and his kingdom we shall not marry, we shall have

[2] It is highly significant that it is expressly with the new law, the interior law of freedom and love, that St. Thomas associates the Lord's counsels (*Summa Theologica*, I–II, q. 108, a. 4). The precept *decides* the course to be taken: "Thou shalt not kill." The counsel *proposes* it (exteriorly through the words of the gospel, interiorly through the calls of charity) and leaves it up to the subject himself to *decide* for himself in the freedom of love: "If you will. . . ." It is a matter of love and of personal prudence in the loveliest sense of the term.

nothing of our own, we shall obey. There is a specific threshold[3] here which constitutes the religious vocation as such. But note well that this definition of the counsels in terms of the religious life does not exhaust their meaning. They make themselves felt with their power of attraction—their spirit in the sense of "inspiration"—in other vocations, for they are bound to charity, which is universal.

Seen in this perspective, the counsels of the Lord belong to the grace of baptism. They are addressed to the whole body. Only through them can the holiness common to the whole Church flourish. Religious—men and women—married lay people, fathers and mothers of families, single people, leaders of industry, all hear them, but they do not put them into practice in the same way. It is the role of religious to manifest their implications in a more striking way in order to recall their demands to their lay brethren. And the laity demonstrate to religious the impressive effects of these same counsels as they live them in their own vocation: devotion, joyful self-denial, generosity, faithfulness, purity of mind and heart. It is a great joy for both to recognize each other in such a real brotherhood.

It is possible that we are living in a time when there is a livelier awareness of these realities. Ah! Grant that we may be grasped by Christ so strongly that our progress towards him will not be interrupted, even if in the human sense our powers are on the decline. What counts is to "know him and

[3] This threshold of religious life is often designated by the expression "the letter of the counsels." By this is meant a will to total, effective detachment. What is called the "spirit of the counsels" is something quite other than a minimized form of them; what is meant, on the contrary, is the counsel in its full strength as it applies universally.

the power of his resurrection . . . becoming like him in his death, that if possible I may attain the resurrection of the dead" (Ph. 3.10). Then we shall lay hold of him even as he has laid hold of us.

9. As Christ Loved the Church

Doubtless you have a mental picture of the closing ceremony of baptism. The celebrant gives the baptized person a lighted candle—symbol of the risen Christ—and says: "Receive this lighted candle . . . so that when the Lord comes for the eternal feast, you may meet him with all the saints . . . and live for ever and ever." Hence it is for a nuptial mystery that baptism destines us. Shall we see how Christian marriage, on one hand, and consecrated virginity, on the other, are two complementary aspects of this same mystery?

The Church, a nuptial mystery

Have you noted that God speaks to us in terms of nuptial love? How far removed this is from dry moralism! God has not been abashed in using the most poignant and deepest thing in human experience to reveal his love to us—the love of man and woman—and what he is saying to us is something like this: "It is not to any tedious ceremony that I am inviting you but to a nuptial mystery. Do you understand this? A marriage mystery."

"The kingdom of heaven may be compared to a king who gave a marriage feast for his son . . ." (Mt. 22.1-4). But in this case God himself is the bridegroom and—what a stunning thing!—the bride is humanity, real humanity in all its poverty, whom he seeks out from afar, whom he rescues, whom he bathes and purifies.

The prophet Hosea, from his own painful experience,[1] tells us how God goes in search of the faithless bride he loves. He takes her from the cultivated land, the gift of her lovers (Hos. 2.12), and leads her into the desert, where he talks tenderly to her; finally, after much conflict, she responds to him again "as in the days of her youth" (Hos. 2.15). There are parallel revelations in Jeremiah and Isaiah: "Thus says the Lord, I remember the devotion of your youth, your love as a bride, how you followed me in the wilderness" (Jr. 2.2); "I have loved you with an everlasting love . . . again you shall adorn yourself with timbrels, and shall go forth in the dance of the merrymakers" (Jr. 31.3–4); "Do not be afraid; you will not be put to shame, for now your creator will be your husband. Does a man cast off the wife of his youth? I did forsake you for a brief moment, but with everlasting love I have taken pity on you" (Is. 54.4, 8). And the Canticle of Canticles sings of a love as strong as death, whose inextinguishable flame is the image of God's jealous love for his people (Ct. 8.6f.). Yes, we may well wonder how it was possible to interpret this ardent revelation in terms of arid moralism. God speaks to us in the accents of love, then and now.

When Christ comes he brings the revelation of this love to its fullness. He made his disciples understand that the Messianic times had come, that these times were like a wedding feast (Mt. 9.15; 22.1–4; 25.1–13), and that he himself was bringing about this marriage by his coming, and even more by his re-

---

[1] It seems evident that in terms of the experience of the prophet Hosea who loved a woman, his faithless wife, God, in the eighth century before our era, revealed these characteristics of a staunch and faithful lover, constantly calling his faithless people back to himself.

demptive death. And after Pentecost it was clear to the apostles, especially John and Paul, that the last word of God's design had been uttered; and so they proclaimed the mystery of the marriage union of Christ with the new humanity which issued from his side, the holy Bride of Christ.

We see this revelation in St. John through the names he gives to Jesus, the Lamb of God, the Bridegroom.[2] By the term Lamb, he means the mysterious figure of the Servant of God in Isaiah (Is. 53.7) who silently bears the sin of men. He also has in mind the paschal lamb whose blood, smeared on the doorposts, preserved the children of Israel when God's exterminating angel passed over the land (Ex. 12.1f.). And when he contemplates the Lord stretched out on the cross, he sees the prophecy fulfilled: Here is the true Lamb of God; "They shall look on him whom they have pierced" (Jn. 19.31–37). He also calls this Lamb the Bridegroom of the new humanity issuing from his side. Such is the central theme of the book of Revelation. The whole history of the world, so often marked by blood and violence, is moving towards a wedding mystery, the marriage of the Lamb and his Bride. History is guided by an unfathomable and mysterious nuptial love: "Let us rejoice and exult and give him the glory, for the marriage of the Lamb has come, and his Bride has made herself ready. . . . Write this: Blessed are those who are invited to the marriage supper of the Lamb" (Rev. 19.7–9). Such is the mystery of the Church.[3]

[2] With regard to the Lamb, see especially Jn. 1.29; 19.36; also Revelation, where the Lamb is the principal symbol (Rev. 5.6; 6, etc.). For the Spouse, see Jn. 3.29 and Rev. 19.7; 21.9, etc.

[3] Let us recall the points on which the analogy of the bride, used to explain the mystery of the Church, is based: (1) Woman came from the side of man, and that is why he loves her; Christ on the cross gave birth to a new humanity saved in his blood, the bride he pre-

We find the same doctrine in St. Paul. Remember the epistle which is read at nuptial Masses: "that he [Christ] might present the church to himself in splendor, without spot or wrinkle or any such thing, that she might be holy and without blemish" (Ep. 5.27).

Thus the mystery of the Church (and the mystery of our lives) is like a marriage mystery. A love is spread out over us whose fidelity, intimacy and fecundity are such that, to reveal it to us, God could find no more eloquent image than that of nuptial love. It is thus that Christ loves the Church, his holy Bride.

Now it is clear why baptism, in introducing us into the heart of the Church's life, leads us into a nuptial mystery as well. As baptized Christians, we must live throughout our lives in this nuptial state—when we are married, through our marriage itself; if we are consecrated to God, through our consecration. In either case it is the same mystery, however different the kinds of life.

This is a great mystery

In the simplicity and sincerity of their love married Christians live the love of Christ present in their home. Their love is deep and intense: joy and sorrow, conflict and repose.

---

pared for himself (Gn. 2.22–24; Ep. 5.26–27). The cross and baptism are her birthplace; the Eucharist is her food. (2) There is a unique quality in the love between the woman and the man: she is bone of his bone. Christ's love for his Church is of this kind: she is born of his heart and the blood issuing from his side. (3) The bride, in her union with the bridegroom, bears him children: Holy Mother Church gives birth to the elect; Christians are born of the unbreakable union of Christ and the Church.

Christ's love is earnest and faithful, strong and full of mercy. And the fact is that there are not two loves here but only one: their human love supernaturalized in its depths; Christ's love penetrating into their human love and redeeming it. All this—which is a great mystery—is brought about very simply, but that does not mean easily. We see it especially in certain Christian homes. There is simplicity and strength in the very atmosphere, giving a consistently human and Christian environment. It is good to love each other this way in Christ.

Fundamentally the history of these homes is that of their love. But their love would not be what it is if Christ were not its constant source: Christ who loved the Church—that is, Christ the Bridegroom, Christ with the love as strong as death. This is in St. Paul's mind when he exclaims: "Husbands, love your wives, as Christ loved the church" (Ep. 5.25). In these homes, even if they are not always aware of it, Christ is living out the mystery of his marriage with the Church. He lives it not with any extraordinary things, but using the very substance of the home: human love, children, trials, joys, weaknesses, the service of men and the Church.

Thus every home of baptized Christians has the mission of manifesting in its own way the reality of the love with which Christ has loved it and with which he loves his Church. May it not be overwhelmed by this mission but find in it the secret of its strength. Let us review those salient characteristics which might be called the "constants" of Christian grace in the home.

First of all there is fidelity, in the sense in which the word might be applied to the flowing of a stream, constant and strong, from an inexhaustible source. God's love, Christ's love, is faithful in this way. We are aware of the question raised by the relation between love and time. Will time nourish love or wear it away? Christ's love is faithful because it transcends time. It is at this source that the married couple are invited to drink. They learn to love with a love stronger than death. "Love never ends" (1 Co. 13.8).

Stronger than their weaknesses, stronger even than ingratitude, Christ's love is patient with that patience which is the strength of hope renewed daily in love. Love like this knows how to endure,[4] to forbear, to forgive. True holiness is found on this road, although the journey may be long.

Christ's love is disinterested. Indeed it is this quality carried to the ultimate extreme which is its essential characterstic. Our own love is always motivated, more or less, by something we hope to receive in return—which is not necessarily sinful. God's love, Christ's love, is not motivated by anything which is to be gained: it is purely a gift, gratuitous, creative. It would be presumptuous to try to imitate it as if we had divine power: we are not creators, and we should learn to receive. Nevertheless Christ teaches us to love as he does in a way that is at once humble and disinterested—when one is the first to love, when one always takes the first step in love.

Christ's love is fruitful. Holy Scripture uses the image "bear fruit." "By this my Father is glorified, that you bear much fruit" (Jn. 15.8). The Church bears fruit for God, and this fruit "abides" (Jn. 15.16). The Christian home has no meaning unless, in the Church, it too bears fruit. That is, far from being turned in on itself, and hence sterile, it must be open, always open. The great tasks of men and those of the Church should be the family's consuming interest. It is not made to live for itself, it is made to live for God, for the

[4] St. Paul's first exclamation, in his hymn to charity, is: "Charity is patient . . ." (1 Co. 13.4).

Church, for men. Of course it should keep and nourish the intimacy without which it is no longer a home, but the grace of baptism impels it to bear fruit for God. Hospitality, openness to others, services extended to our fellow men, joining in the common struggles for God's kingdom—all this nourishes and fortifies the Christian home. It is perhaps by this sign above all that our contemporaries shall know that the kingdom of God has already come into the midst of us.

This history of love in the depths of the life of baptized Christians will not be made without the cross; indeed the cross will be found in all homes in which families are learning to live their baptized life, like the presence of Christ in their midst. But where Christ's cross is, there is his love and his Holy Spirit also. And St. Paul tells us what its fruits are: love, joy, peace, patience, and so on (Ga. 5.22). So it is that already on earth baptized Christians live in their marriage the marriage union of Christ with his Church, a union which is intimate and profound. And together they press on towards a love which will have no end.

Like a pure virgin

Those who are consecrated to God live the same mystery, but in a different way. Married Christians live it in and through their love itself; the consecrated, in offering the sacrifice of their human love to God, purely for love of him. But the source is the same for the love raised above earthly things and the love in earthly marriage. It is this nuptial love of Christ which overflows in the hearts of both; in the former, vivifying, purifying and nourishing their love for each other; in the latter, making it possible for them to offer the sacrifice

of their human love without psychological difficulties or dis-
content. In either way of life we must be filled to overflowing with the nuptial love of Christ.

This love of Christ is also virginal, in the case of married
people as well as of religious, though in a different sense in
each. St. Paul exclaimed: "I wish you would bear with me
in a little foolishness. Do bear with me! I feel a divine jealousy
for you, for I betrothed you to Christ to present you as a pure
bride" (2 Co. 11.1–2). To whom does he say that? To our
fathers in the Faith, the early Christians of Corinth, married
or unmarried (1 Co. 7), some of whom had not even been
behaving themselves (1 Co. 5). He spoke to them of these
marvellous things because of their baptism itself. Through
their baptism a certain virginal quality was infused into their
souls; they belonged in a unique way to Christ. They had
been dearly purchased (1 Co. 6.15–20). Some part of their
hearts was reserved for God alone. In the most united home
each of the married partners is a high mystery known to God
alone, and this, far from hindering their love for each other,
nourishes it in a hidden way.

Now, perhaps, we have a better understanding of the doctrine. The life of men with God in its depths is within the
grasp of a mystery which God himself has revealed as nuptial.
God loves men with the ardor, the "jealousy," the strength,
of a husband. He has loved, he loves, them to the point of
having shed his blood that they might be born. Hence he is
above all the Bridegroom of his people; this people has cost
him dearly; it has issued from his pierced side, as the first
woman came from the side of man, and thus it is "bone of
his bone and flesh of his flesh." This "people" is not a meta-
physical concept. Look up to heaven and think of those who

are in it: Francis of Assisi and Father de Foucauld, Thérèse of Lisieux and Teresa of Avila. Look round about us on earth and see Christian men and women living as best they can in Christ. This people is a communion, it is a Church; and this Church, unceasingly born of Christ, is his Bride, through whom he accomplishes everything.

Baptism introduces us into the very life of this holy Bridegroom living its mystery in all of us, and in this mystery virginity and nuptial love are united. Virginal: there is in the heart of every baptized Christian (and of every man, as a matter of fact) an element known to God alone and made for him alone. Nuptial: the heart of every man is called by God to a love in which he will find his consummation. This mystery in which virginal and nuptial love are united is lived out in a complementary way by married Christians and consecrated religious. The former live it through their love itself; the latter, through offering to God the sacrifice of this love, in order to bind themselves to the Lord with undivided devotion (1 Co. 7.35). The intensity, the depth, of the love between married people bears witness to the intensity and the depth of God's love. The intensity, the purity, of the love of consecrated religious bears witness to the intensity and purity of God's love. Thérèse of Lisieux lived out a marriage mystery in Carmel. In their way of life, blessed and sanctified by God, her parents had lived out this same mystery before her; and now, reunited in heaven, we dare hope that they are celebrating the eternal nuptial mystery of the Lamb in a manner which surpasses the imagination.[5]

[5] The development which this doctrine should have is outside the scope of this chapter. Let us say simply this: with married people, love, through the power of the sacrament, is the efficacious sign of

Put into words, these realities seem abstruse. Lived out, they become simple through grace. Think of our Christian homes, of our children, called by God to his service; cast our minds back over our personal history, and we shall see, through faith, that we are living out a high mystery of love.

"As Christ loved the Church. . . ." "Love never ends."

---

the nuptial love of Christ, who manifests himself and acts through their love itself; consecrated religious offer to God the sacrifice of this love in order to embrace, at once and directly, the "reality," namely, the nuptial love of Christ which will never end and in which we all shall reach consummation.

Part II
IN THE IMAGE OF CHRIST

10. He Who Has Seen Me Has Seen the Father

What an astounding statement! The very St. John who declares on several occasions that no one has ever seen God (Jn. 1.18; 6.46; 1 Jn. 4.12) puts these simple and yet extraordinary words into Christ's mouth: "He who has seen me has seen the Father." No man has ever seen the Father; but look at Jesus, live with him, and little by little you will learn who the Father is. To the men of all times, God speaks through Christ. And it is required of us Christians that we should be signs speaking of Christ, who has not lost all his power over our contemporaries, even though his features, unhappily, seem to have become obscure in their minds.

No one has ever seen God

It has often been noted that the true God manifests himself as at once a God whose name is beyond utterance and a God who is in the innermost depths of the heart. He is a holy God, and we bend our knees before him. He is a God who is near, so near that at each moment we can meet him in the most hidden recesses of our selves. This may be the Face which our contemporaries are searching for without knowing it: a God who shall be truly God, a God who shall be really their God, whose presence shall transform their whole lives.

To Moses, who asked God to show him his face, God said: "You cannot see my face; for man shall not see me and live" (Ex. 33.20).[1] Here, no doubt, we have the point of departure of the highest vocation of Judeo-Christian mysticism. God is a hidden God in his transcendence; no man has ever seen him. But let us strive to grasp the meaning of this word transcendence as it applies to the God of revelation. It does not mean a frozen solitude, as though one might say: "God, if he exists, cannot concern himself with man." It is a *religious* transcendence which is involved—that is, a mystery, at once ineffable and attractive, before which man falls on his knees because of an obscure intimation that this tremendous God is at the same time *his* God.

The biblical word which expresses this aspect of the divine mystery is "holiness." God is holy, thrice holy. Let us remove the word from the category of morality here. God is holy in this sense, that in his own order of existence he is totally inaccessible and of his nature ineffable. Hence there is in the soul of man, made in his image, one point made for him alone—virginal—which must be constantly guarded and purified. The idol is that which takes the place of God at this point of his soul. Therefore before God every man experiences an intense need for purification. He feels instinctively that this is how he will find him. God said to Moses: "Do not come near; put off your shoes from your feet, for the place on which you are standing is holy ground" (Ex. 3.5). And when in his vision Isaiah cried, "I am a man of unclean lips," one of the seraphim flew to him, having in his hand a burning

---

[1] The book of Exodus is without doubt the book of the Old Testament in which the most forceful expression is given to the holiness and the glory of the true God, which cannot be reconciled with the worship of any idol whatsoever (cf. Ex. 3; 33.18–23; 34.5–9).

coal with which he touched the prophet's mouth and said, "Behold, this has touched your lips; your guilt is taken away, and your sin forgiven."[2]

But the startling thing is that already, in the Old Testament, this unfathomable God speaks to man, this holy God calls man to tell him his Name; this God whom no man has seen involves himself in man's individual and collective history. When he manifests himself, he always uses much the same words: "Do not fear," or again, "I am with you."[3] He is in the heights of heaven, and yet at the same time he is aware of every heartbeat of the man he calls. He is truly a holy God, and he is God-with-us.

Now it is precisely these two features which Jesus "fulfills" for us, but in such a prodigious manner as our hearts could never have hoped for. With Christ, God is now in the midst of us. He remains indeed the holy God whom no one has ever seen, but at the same time, in his unfathomable compassion, he is the Love who became a servant and who loved us to the end (Jn. 13.1).

I made known to them thy name

This is how Jesus sums up his mission at the end of his life (Jn. 17.26). He was thinking, surely, of this Name above all

[2] Is. 6.5–8. Cf. Dt. 4.24. God manifests himself under the aspect of a tongue of fire. He is called a "jealous" God who does not tolerate divided hearts—that is, idols. And this is because he is God and because he wants man to preserve in his heart a burning sense of the fact that he is the Only One. This is God's glory, and for man the secret of truth, freedom and joy.

[3] These words appear constantly in the Bible. To take only two, particularly striking, examples, cf. Moses' calling: "I will be with you" (Ex. 3.12) and the angel's words to Mary: "Do not be afraid. The Lord is with you" (Lk. 1.28).

other names with which the history of the Bible is filled. To
know the name of God—what does this mean? It means to
savor it in one's heart and to utter it with infinite reverence.
Now even on earth one is on first-name terms only with
friends, usually close friends. So, if a man utters the name of
God in his heart, if he utters it in a certain way, it is because
God has made himself known to him and has become *his* God.
Jesus' whole mission—the whole mission of the Church—is
to make the name of God known in this way, so that little by
little the uttering of this sacred name becomes as natural to
us as breathing. Then it is hallowed, then his kingdom comes.

I have manifested thy name to the men whom thou gavest me
out of the world (Jn. 17.6). I made known to them thy name,
and I will make it known (Jn. 17.26).

The whole teaching and the whole life of Christ seem to
be dominated by this Other One whom he calls his Father and
whom he makes known to us. We must let ourselves be in-
structed by him on this point, which surpasses all others in
importance. Only on this condition shall we have God in our
hearts.

He teaches us first through his words. We must love to read
and reread them. Only thus shall we become his disciples.

When you pray, pray like this: "Our Father. . . ." Holy
Father, keep them in thy name, those whom thou hast given to
me. . . . And forgive us our debts, as we also have forgiven our
debtors. . . . The hour is coming when the true worshipers will
worship the Father in spirit and truth. . . . No one is good but
God alone. . . .

Each day, gathered around the altar, we can, if we will, let ourselves be taught by Christ and, with him, repeat the words in which the name of the Father is made known; words in which each petition, flowing slowly into our minds, describes an aspect of our God—his holiness, his kingdom, his will, the bread he wants to give to his children, his forgiveness and the deliverance from evil. It is thus that, little by little, we become Christians.

Jesus also reveals the Father to us through his life. The more one reads and ponders the gospels, the more one sees Christ as oriented towards, grasped and ruled by, the One he calls his Father. He wanted to show us thus, through his humanity, what a man is like who lives for God, is consecrated to him. Most assuredly we see Christ living for us, but not for an instant do we see him leaving God. Listen, again, to some of his words:

Did you not know that I must be in my Father's house? . . . My food is to do the will of him who sent me. . . . I am always with the Father because I always do what is pleasing to him. . . . Father, not my will but thine. . . . Father, into thy hands I commend my spirit. . . .

He loved us to the end

Through his teaching and through his life, Christ above all speaks to us of God, of a holy God. But at the same time, in a very striking way, he brings us the revelation that God loves us. "He who has seen me has seen the Father." Let us look at Christ, and we shall see in him the face of God's love on earth. Here we shall recall only two of its features.

When God loves us he humbles himself without debasing himself. It is a characteristic of his on which his saints have meditated at length and which has converted them little by little.

Christ Jesus, who, though he was in the form of God, did not count equality with God a thing to be grasped, but emptied himself, taking the form of a servant, being born in the likeness of men (Ph. 2.6).

All the saints have contemplated him as he "rose from supper, laid aside his garments, and girded himself with a towel. Then he poured water into a basin, and began to wash the disciples' feet" (Jn. 13.4–5). Do you want to know who the holy God, hidden in the clouds, is? Look at Christ washing his disciples' feet. There he is, in his dignity as the Lord, restoring men, by his example, to the one way of the truth which makes us free; on this way he shows us not only the true face of God but the real meaning of everything else as well—this truth which is summed up in becoming a servant out of love. "Let the greatest among you become as the youngest, and the leader as one who serves" (Lk. 22.26).

When God loves us, he loves us to the end. It is evident that we cannot give reasons to explain the mystery of the cross. In our effort to comprehend it, we must always go back to the words with which St. John throws light on the passion: "Before the feast of the Passover, when Jesus knew that his hour had come to depart out of this world to the Father, having loved his own who were in the world, he loved them to the end" (Jn. 13.1). Plainly it is in the context of love—love which endures to the end—that the evangelist wished to place our Lord's passion.

The wellspring of Christian holiness is always a specific kind of "love to the end," which is the enemy of self-satisfaction and impels the lover to give up his life. "For the love of Christ controls us," St. Paul said (2 Co. 5.14). God makes himself known to us interiorly and "urges" us in a variety of ways. Apostles, contemplatives, priests, laymen—there is no kind of Christian who is not conscious, at one time or another, of this pressure impelling him to "lose himself" in love. And the source of this extraordinary daily impulse of love is always a look towards Christ: "He who has seen me has seen the Father." It is always by looking at Christ that we learn what the love of God is in practice.

But Christ cannot be separated from his Church. He is God's Sign par excellence; but in his mystical body he is a sign growing constantly larger through time by adding members to itself—adding men, ourselves. Amongst the nations who do not know the true God it is the whole Christ, Head and members—the living Church—which is the Sign of God. She is this sign to the extent that she is transparent to the gospel and to Christ. The immense efforts towards renewal being made at the present time, owing to the Council, should fill us with hope and excitement. But we must not forget that we ourselves are the Church. We, therefore, are asked to renew ourselves as well—that is, to become so closely united to Christ that he shines through our lives, even if we do not speak of him in words.

What can we do to become, in union with Christ and the Church, signs which are eloquent of his presence? First, let us have in our hearts a really consuming sense of God's holiness. Then, let us live out in our lives the mystery of his love, which led him to wash the feet of his disciples and to be raised on the cross for us.

For what God wanted to make known to the men of all times is that he is at the same time a God whom no one can see and a God of love: "No man has ever seen God; if we love one another, God abides in us and his love is perfected in us" (1 Jn. 4.12). It is this that Christ came to tell us and to fulfill.

11. I Am the Truth

In the biblical sense the word "truth" represents a richer, a more total, reality than is conveyed by its dictionary meaning. As it is used in our language it implies an intellectual attitude, a mental certitude, an assent of the intellect. But in Scripture an adherence of one's whole being is implied; it is a question of entering into the truth, of oneself *becoming* it. Hence God is not called simply "the truth." More concretely, more mysteriously, he is called "the One who is true," the one who sets himself against darkness and idolatry.[1]

When our Lord says, "I am the truth," we must take this term in the same absolute and total sense. Christ is the truth in the sense that he sums up and incarnates the fullness of revelation. He is also the truth in the sense of being the true One in whom there is neither darkness nor falsehood, in whom the truth of all things resides. Let us ask God in fervent prayer for the grace so to enter into the truth of Christ that our brethren outside the faith may feel, in their encounters with us, that he is the truth for us.

God of truth . . .

In the Old Testament it is in opposition to idols that God reveals himself as the true God. By idols we mean not only

[1] Cf. 1 Jn. 5.20; Jn. 17.3.

the false gods of paganism but also the "idols of the heart," that is, the God-substitutes and the deformations of the true God which set themselves up against faith and true love— not only the Baals but, even more, money, human respect, power, and so on. Religious men of all times have been persistently preoccupied with the problem of guarding their hearts against the incursion of idols. So much so that it is in relation to the false gods so real in the minds of men that the true God reveals himself; it is through comparison with the falseness of these idols that his veracious characteristics become apparent: the idols fall, God still stands; the idols turn to dust, God is the rock; the idols are all vanity, God does not deceive us.[2] In other words, the idols represent the outer darkness, the lie; God is the "one who is true"; the man who has found him is not straying and lost, he is in the truth.

As well as the "one who is true," God is called "the faithful."[3] This essential attribute of the God of revelation is based on the Covenant and the Promises. The fact of the matter is that God has spoken, has made mysterious and boundless promises to men, and it is with reference to these that he is called faithful. From Abraham to Jesus, sacred history is full of the proclamation and the fulfillment of these promises. And this does not come to an end with Jesus. With him and with

---

[2] The Bible uses the terms "dust," "vanity," "nothingness," "the lie," "the darkness," and so on, to designate the idols opposed to the true God.

[3] Faithfulness is an essential attribute of the God of revelation. He presents himself as faithful and full of mercy, faithful to his promises; he is indefatigable in seeking out the faithless ones who have gone far astray (cf. Ex. 34.5–9; Hos. 2.8–18; 21–25). Jesus Christ is presented as the great example of fidelity (cf. 2 Co. 1.18–20; 2 Tm. 2.13; Rev. 1.5, etc.).

the Holy Spirit (called specifically the Spirit of the Promise),[4] the fulfillment continues in the history of the Church and of the world; in history taken collectively and in our personal histories.[5] God is called a God of truth in the sense that all down the centuries he is unswervingly faithful to his promises in face of the constant infidelity of men.

And yet men are themselves called to become faithful and true. There are shadows and lies in men's souls, but there is truth there as well. In their deepest hearts there is enough truth for them to be in harmony with God. It is then that they will become really themselves and rediscover the truth of things. The fact is that God has given them a heart capable of knowing him. We know the great promise made to Jeremiah: "I shall give them a heart to know that I am the Lord."[6] This religious knowledge of God is given to us in the measure that our hearts become "true" according to God's standards. Such is our "new heart," our "heart of flesh," our "heart created according to God in the holiness of truth."[7] We should

[4] Like Yahweh in the Old Testament, Jesus makes promises (cf., among other references, Mk. 10.29–30; Mt. 28.20). The Church lives from them, and their fulfillment sustains her faith. The Holy Spirit is called the Spirit of the Promise in the sense that the pouring forth on earth of the Spirit in its plenitude after Christ's resurrection fulfills the divine promises (Ac. 2.33); also in the sense that his manifestation in the Church constitutes the earnest, the first fruits, of eternal life already begun (2 Co. 1.22; Ep. 1.14; etc.).

[5] Thus the effective realization of our vocation is the fulfillment in us of the promises of the faithful God, whose gifts are irrevocable and in whom all things work for good for those who love him (Rm. 11.29; 8.28).

[6] Jer. 24.7. See the note accompanying this verse in the Jerusalem Bible.

[7] These diverse expressions denote our most intimate spiritual center —spirit and love—insofar as God visits it and re-creates it according

constantly ask ourselves whether the reason that we have such
a slight acquaintance with God may not be that we are not
sufficiently true-hearted, with the truth which comes from
him.

No man ever spoke as this man speaks

Our Lord takes his place in this biblical tradition which
we have just briefly summarized, but, as always, he "fulfills"
it beyond all expectations.

He presents himself first of all as the truth in the sense that
he has a unique authority over our minds and hearts. An
intimate and mysterious authority such as this is of its nature
supernatural.[8] It stimulates the act of faith. Hence it is normal
that the unbeliever should not yet experience it, and in this
case we can only await God's hour with deep reverence. God
alone judges the heart.

And yet even now Christ's word goes a long way for such
a man, and here his religious history comes into play. We
recall that Gide remarked, in his *Journal*, that he believed

---

to his truth. For the "new heart" see Ezek. 36.26; Jer. 31.31. For the
"new nature created after the likeness of God in true righteousness
and holiness" see Ep. 4.24.

[8] The word "authority" does not express very clearly the reality
which is the cause of our faith. We say in theology that the authority
of God revealing is the formal motive of faith, understanding this
word in the sense of an *intimate*—not exterior—authority, such as the
author of all truth alone can have over the center of our being. The
same holds true in the case of Christ. His person and his word carry
their supernatural "proof" with them. They kindle faith and sustain it.
St. Paul attributes this role more specifically to the Holy Spirit, "bearing witness with our spirit" that God is our Father and that Jesus is
Lord (Rm. 8.16; cf. 1 Co. 12.3).

Christ was God not because he said so but because of *what* he said. Yet Christ as much as said that he was God through his attitudes and words; but more than this, what he said enters the heart, and some day or other it reveals itself as the Word of Life, the Word of God. As Bergson remarked in his *Two Sources of Morality and Religion,* even those who went to the length of denying Jesus' historicity could not prevent the Sermon on the Mount from figuring in the gospel along with other divine sayings. Thus, for the unbeliever with an upright heart, the word of Jesus often has even now an extraordinary resonance, whose depth he himself is unable to grasp; and it is by following this word that he may, perhaps, one day be led into the Faith.

As for us believers, we rejoice in bearing witness: the word of Jesus has changed our lives. If we let ourselves be converted by it, we have experiential knowledge that it is truth and life. The "disciple"—a word so dear to the gospel, and in particular to St. John[9]—is he who receives the word into his heart and keeps it. It lives in him and changes him. Fundamentally, our great reason for believing is that through living the word of Jesus we have experienced its truth as one incomparably surpassing all our human verities. We could say, with St. Peter: "Lord, to whom shall we go? You have the words of eternal life" (Jn. 6.68). And with the officers sent by the Sanhedrin to apprehend Jesus we might acknowledge that "no man ever spoke like this man" (Jn. 7.46).

[9] In the gospels, the disciple is one who listens to the word of Jesus in the sense of accepting and believing it. He does not change the word, it changes him. It becomes his law and his life. This is very marked in St. John, the "disciple whom Jesus loves," whose life was one of continuous contemplation. He "dwells" in Jesus.

I am the truth

But now let us come to the heart of the matter, to this phrase which astonishes us, the way so many of Jesus' remarks do: "Believe in God, believe also in me . . . I am the truth" (Jn. 14.1–6).

For the sake of brevity we shall limit ourselves to the two interpretations mentioned in the beginning of this chapter.

First, Christ is the truth in the sense that he expresses and incarnates the fulfillment of revelation. He produced no inventions, he unveiled none of the secrets of nature, of philosophy or politics. But he told us all that God wanted to make known to us. He revealed the Father to us and told us that we are loved by him; he himself loved us, died for us, was raised from the dead and gave us his Spirit. In him and with him we form one single body, the holy Vine of God growing in the midst of the world and bearing fruit for God which abides.[10]

For St. John especially, Christ the Truth is Christ Word of the Father, who declares the Father to us and gives us understanding of all wonders of wisdom and love which reside in the Father.[11] Let us listen to him:

And we know that the Son of God has come and has given us understanding, to know him who is true; and we are in him who

[10] The revelation of Christ taken as a whole soon formed a body of doctrine in the Church, a creed. Our fathers in the Faith did not have simply a generalized faith. Already St. Paul sets forth the Christian Faith in an ensemble of essential affirmations (see 1 Co. 15.1–8; cf. 1 Jn. 2.23, etc.), a rough sketch of the Apostles' Creed, or the *Regula fidei.*

[11] Jn. 14.6.7. See Father Mollat's note on this in the Jerusalem Bible.

is true, in his Son Jesus Christ. This is the true God and eternal life.[12]

> And this is eternal life, that they know thee the only true God, and Jesus Christ whom thou hast sent (Jn. 17.3).

In this first sense—as the fullness of God's revelation—faith in Christ means fundamentally a sharing through him of the hidden knowledge of the Father (Jn. 15.15). That is to say, faith tends to be contemplative. It is so constituted as to be nourished by light. Without this nourishment it becomes anaemic and reveals itself as powerless to convert the world to the revealed Christ.[13]

In the second place, Christ is truth in the sense that those who believe in him enter, little by little, into the whole truth. This is another aspect of the faith and the truth of Christ. By faith we not only receive and accept the truth; we ourselves become "of the truth." This aspect is particularly dear to St. John. To hear the voice of Christ, we must already be "of the truth" (Jn. 18.37–38). In order to believe in him, we must already belong to his flock (Jn. 10.26). Hence faith pre-supposes that God should bring man into interior harmony with Jesus. However, he will do this only on the basis of man's good will, a good will growing ceaselessly throughout life. We can, of course, arrive at faith through study, but we shall do it far more readily by attuning ourselves to truth. "He who does what is true comes to the light" (Jn. 3.21).

[12] 1 Jn. 5.20. This fundamental text must be pondered at length.
[13] This may be the main reason why the vague faith of many Christians is not very contagious. They "believe," but they do not live in union with the Father and his Son, Jesus Christ. They have no comprehension of what they believe.

St. John teaches us, even more precisely, that we enter into the truth by following the twofold commandment of Christ: to believe in his name and to love one another (1 Jn. 3.23; 2.21–22; 3.19). God's truth is, then, a reality for those who believe and love. This twofold wealth is at the same time a gift and a disposition. Here we are brought face to face with the mystery of grace and the mystery of ourselves. To be counted among those who believe is a gift of God, but it is also the beginning of our response to him. For, at a greater depth than discursive reason, our "heart" utters a secret yes or no to him. It accepts or refuses him. It is already in the world of faith, even if the mind lags behind it. "To everyone who has will more be given" (Lk. 19.26). God, who was the initiator, completes his own work, and faith then becomes a matter of collaboration between God and man. And what we can say about faith in its beginning we can equally say of love. "By this [that is, our love] we shall know that we are of the truth" (1 Jn. 3.19). Through loving one another we enter into Christ's truth and prepare ourselves for an increase of faith in him. "No man has ever seen God; if we love one another, God abides in us and his love is perfected in us" (1 Jn. 4.12).

It seems that at their baptism the early Christians used to sing the hymn of which a fragment is preserved in the Epistle to the Ephesians:

> Awake, O sleeper, and arise from the dead,
> and Christ shall give you light (Ep. 5.14).

How this verse, shot through with hope, could be applied to our contemporaries! Many of them have fallen into sleep of all sorts. They hardly, it seems, believe in truth any more. And yet, as soon as the voice of Christ resounds in them, striking a certain chord in their being—this note of truth which we, the believers, have the mission to make understood—they thrill to it. And the history of the gospel repeats itself. Those who are "of the truth" hear his voice.

12. Blessed Are You!

The gospel of Jesus is fundamentally the gospel of "happiness"—an evocative and ambiguous word which awakens endless reverberations in the human heart. Assuredly the happiness revealed by Christ and lived by him and his is strangely different from that which the world talks about and which we often hope for secretly in our hearts. Nevertheless this great word flashes out in the gospel, from beginning to end; and perhaps it is because we are of such little faith that we dare not believe that this happiness will one day be ours, that it can be ours even now.

O Lord, open our hearts to the happiness you want to give us!

We do not want happiness

This is the cry of so many of our contemporaries, who fear that the word is a snare and a delusion. Thus, they want happiness (with a small h) "such as one can find on earth"; but they more or less reject Happiness (with a capital H)—this "Christian" word which, they say, has alienated so many men from society, in a quest for something quite outside their human situation. Doubtless it will take us a long time to discover the ways the hearts of our non-Christian brothers take in their approach to the true happiness which they perceive obscurely and desire in spite of themselves. In any case, there is no doubt that if the Christian message is to find acceptance, it must be related more or less consciously to the hope for happiness which we all have within us. If we find our happiness in trivialities, if our thirst is too slight, God's word will leave us indifferent.

We know that it is always in relation to our thirst for happiness, for the abundance which quenches all thirst, that Christian thought has sought to present revelation, and this from St. Augustine to St. Thomas Aquinas[1] and from Newman to Blondel. Under a diversity of forms the process has been the same: search the heart of man until the signs of his fundamental orientation are discerned—namely, a thirst not only for pleasure and comfort but still more a thirst for a full and satisfying happiness which no created thing can provide. It is here, in this appetite for happiness, that Christian thought has seen our "openness," as persons, to God; it is here that he makes his influence felt, when he is little by little becoming a God who has a real relation to our "hearts," to our happiness.

On the face of it, our non-Christian contemporaries seem to be more modest in their aims. They use more moderate words

[1] For St. Augustine, for example, it is the famous phrase from his *Confessions*: "Thou hast made us for thyself, and our hearts are restless until they rest in thee."

For St. Thomas, on the other hand, the whole of morality is rooted in the "appetite for beatitude"—that is, blessedness. It is in our intellectual nature that he discerns "eyes made to see," and it is reasoning from this nature fundamentally fashioned for vision that he establishes an "expectation," a "natural desire to see God." Specific Christian revelation ("Blessed are the pure of heart, for they will see God") fulfills this expectation to infinity. They will see God; they will be satisfied, happy, blessed.

—pleasure, comfort, social betterment—or words which suggest a greater disinterestedness—social justice, human progress, and so on. Depending on the kind of people they are, they would say, glibly: "Not happiness but pleasure"; "Human progress rather than happiness"; "Social justice before happiness"; and so on.[2] And it will be our place to show them, through our words and even more through our actions, that we reject neither pleasure nor human progress nor social justice but that, however noble and fraught with hope these words may be, we thirst for an even deeper reality: that of a right relation of our souls with God. Happy is the man who is in God's hands and who finds in these hands the power to engage in his earthly and heavenly combat, and the purgation of his joys. It is for this happiness—personal and fraternal, divine and human—that we thirst, on our own behalf and for those we love.

[2] It might be said that systems of morality more or less bound up with Christianity, or capable of being related to it, are characterized by a morality of happiness, not happiness taken in the egoistic sense but in that of an objective plenitude in right relation to the human spirit. All Christian thinkers have striven to bring to light in detail the disproportion which exists between the deepest needs and aspirations of the human spirit and its present condition. And it is in relation to this incongruity that they are able to show to best advantage the infinite and and gratuitous fullness of Christian truth: God loves you, and one day you will be with him. It must be admitted that, if it is misapprehended, this morality can serve as a cloak for personal egotism, and even give it a religious sanction. In that case it presents an obstacle to what our contemporaries are demanding with such violence: a social justice based on a deeper sense of brotherhood. From this point of view it is easy to understand their rejection of our philosophy—"Not happiness but justice."

Blessed is he who trusts in God

Slowly, in the course of Holy Scripture, God has trained us in the art of happiness. He did not wean us too soon; he did not deprive us of legitimate earthly blessings. One could even draw from the Bible a very human—very "carnal," Pascal would say—picture of the happiness the devout Israelite was expecting from his God: handsome sons and daughters, full granaries, numerous flocks.[3] The inspired author is even specific: a good king, a sensible wife, honestly acquired wealth, and so on (Qo. [Ecclesiastes] 10.16; Si. [Ecclesiasticus] 25.1; 31.8, etc.). None of these things are unimportant. But one easily sees the danger: one can be degraded by them. We are familiar with Pascal's thought on this subject. The Jews, having grown old in their carnal illusions, were expecting fertile lands, a solidly constructed temple, and a Messiah coming to consecrate it. In their expectation of a too human, nationalistic kind of happiness, they were dull of heart. In Jesus they did not recognize the Messiah, so true is it that our concept of God is molded by the quality of the happiness we are looking forward to, consciously or unconsciously.

Therefore, as early as Old Testament times, we are witness to a deep purgation being carried on by God in the thirst for happiness of his faithful people. There are, in particular, the psalms of "Yahweh's poor." In the midst of their most severe trial, exile and deportation, the men of faith will proclaim trust in God as an absolute good. Above earthly goods, not negligible in themselves and always to be sought, there is a

---

[3] Cf. Ps. 112.2–3; 128; 144.12–15.

Good, a Happiness, which nothing can take away: that of being in God's hands. What delight, what sweetness there is, in being with God. Blessed are those who dwell in his house. Blessed are those who walk in his paths. He is the God of our hearts. "My flesh and my soul shout for joy in your presence, O Lord."[4]

This transformation in the devout Israelite's concept of the happiness he awaited and hoped for is so real that exegetes see in this experience of religious happiness the first seeds of the revelation of "eternal life." It was by tasting God's goodness in their hearts, and the sweetness of being in his hands, that believers progressively received the revelation of the true nature of eternal life: that they will never be separated from God and will, one day, be with him for ever. "Eternal life," or life with God in the happiness proper to him, is something different in kind—infinitely simpler and infinitely higher— than "immortality." Not only shall we not die, but "we shall always be with the Lord."[5]

Look at him

When the beloved Son becomes man, he will show us by example and teaching wherein our happiness lies. Look long

[4] Here we find the loveliest echoes of the soul of Israel, echoes which the Church has made her own. Cf. Is. 40.15–18; Ps. 2.12; 84.3–6; 146.5–9; 73.25. Note especially the last of these psalms. In a more profound sense than the goods which he affords, it is God himself whom the man of faith hopes for: "Whom have I in heaven but thee? And there is nothing upon earth that I desire besides thee."

[5] Such is the simplest definition of heaven: "And so we shall always be with the Lord" (cf. 1 Th. 4.17). Plato, however great he was, attained only to the concept of the immortality of the soul. He did not have the advantage of the revelation of a God with whom it is good to dwell.

at him in his hidden life and in his public life, and you will learn, little by little, wherein happiness consists.

He was not abashed by our human joys; he lived them, he blessed them. He had a mother; he had a father, who, if he did not give him life, did give him his fatherly love, his work, his care. He had a home, a house. He had friends. He wept over the death of one of them. He loved with his human heart. He rejected nothing in his Father's creation—the sun, the wind, the crops. He trusted men. He loved one named John, another called Peter, and with full knowledge of their fragility and weakness he entrusted his Church to them. Even on the cross he took thought for his mother, who stood there until he breathed his last.

Yes, most assuredly, when we gaze on the sacred humanity of Jesus we know for certain that he did not condemn our nature but that he became human as no other man can ever be.

But at the same time we see that his happiness was centered on something infinitely above the human level. When he was twelve years old, his mother already was aware of it: "Did you not know that I must be in my Father's house?" (Lk. 2.49). Poor human woman—so fully a woman, too; she had to learn to accept the fact that her Son's happiness was something quite other than anything she had envisaged; above all, learn to accept the fact that she herself had not the power to give it to him fully. He was "from God." He was on the way to God. There was his whole life. Through his consecrated humanity he was teaching her, and he teaches us, in divinely simple words, wherein is his peace and wherein ours should be; about the one thing necessary, the only thing necessary—to remain in the Father's hands, come what may; to suffer for his kingdom; to love all those whom he loves, and most especially those he entrusts to us. "You will be scattered

... and will leave me alone; yet I am not alone, for the Father is with me" (Jn. 16.32). It is impossible to read, to ponder, the gospels without recognizing clearly that it is in the Father that his life, his happiness, is centered, even though he rejects none of our simple and real human joys on that account.

There was the night of the passion, on which he elected to share the anguish which comes to us in our "nights" of suffering: abandoned by his friends and betrayed by one of them, denied by another; undergoing destitution, thirst, seemingly abandonment by God, human death. And yet from all this what peace emerges. When we leaf through the gospels, turning the pages dealing with the passion slowly, it is his words on the cross, so full of peace, which stand out: "Forgive them, for they know not what they do. . . . Today you will be with me in paradise. . . . I thirst. . . . Behold, your mother. . . . It is consummated. . . . Father, into thy hands I commit my spirit."[6]

And on the third day he rose from the dead. Divine joy without measure—which had never withdrawn from his soul[7] —now pervaded his body, still bearing the marks of his wounds on hands and feet and side, and he was glorified (Jn. 17.1). And now whole and entire in his sacred humanity, "hidden in God" (Col. 3.3), he is happy, blessed, and he fills with happiness without end all those whom he has redeemed with his blood.

---

[6] The words "My God, my God, why hast thou forsaken me?", so poignant that all three synoptists have reported them, are the beginning of a psalm of trust and abandonment (Ps. 22).

[7] Mysterious though it may be, the Catholic faith teaches that even on the cross Christ had the beatific vision in his soul—the divine source of his joy. However, this did not take away his suffering.

Blessed are you . . .

Have we now a better understanding of what is called the paradox of the Beatitudes? It is possible to say that Jesus' teaching begins and ends with this: "He taught them, saying: Blessed. . . . Blessed. . . ." (Mt. 5.1). Wholly in his Father's hands, his own happiness made fast, he declares who those are who are in the Father's favor, who have entered into the truth. Even though the happiness he proclaims runs counter to everything the world recognizes as such, the "little, unimportant people" have an intuition of it and recognize it in the depths of their hearts.

"Blessed are the poor in spirit . . . blessed are the meek . . . blessed are those who mourn . . . blessed are those who hunger and thirst for righteousness . . . blessed are the merciful . . . blessed are the pure in heart . . . blessed are the peacemakers . . . blessed are those who are persecuted for righteousness sake. . . ." Christ declares them all blessed in face of heaven and earth, for they are really in God's hands. They are God's. They are on the way to God. They have found the truth. They are "of the truth" of the Lamb, and hence they follow him wherever he goes (Rev. 14.4).

They will see God

"They will see God"—these words blaze out of Christian revelation. The Old Testament could never go as far as that. Quite the contrary: "No one has ever seen God" (Jn. 1.18; cf. Ex. 33). Jesus was the first to utter these extraordinary words, in connection with one of the Beatitudes—that which concerns the pure in heart: "Blessed are the pure in heart, for they shall see God." The only ones who will see him are those who have become—in this life or in the other—pure in heart. St. John echoes this promise of Jesus in his First Epistle: One day "we shall be like him, for we shall see him as he is" (1 Jn. 3.2). Perhaps our word "vision" falls far short of the mysterious reality of our glorious seeing in heaven. On earth, anything we see is set at a distance from us, outside our minds; in eternal life there is no distance between God and us at all: our seeing is communion in its fullness. Hence Christian thought has added an adjective to the word "vision"—"beatific," giving bliss. Happiness, fullness, satiation, joy, tears of joy—all these words together fail to convey the sense of the happiness which awaits us, which God gratuitously prepares for those who love him (1 Col. 2.9). Yes, in the depths of our hearts it seems to us incredible that we are destined for this happiness; we are unable to comprehend the fact that God has created us to be happy with a happiness that is immense, unlimited.

Our Lord himself will be our happiness. Does this mean that there will be no human element in it? The Church is serene in this regard, asking us to learn to leave the question up to God. With the greatest of her doctors she holds, first of all, that God is all-sufficing, and that the knowledge of the blessed in heaven is not had in our own light but in the light which comes from God. We shall, then, experience a transcendence of ourselves, a radical change in our too human attitudes. But at the same time the Church reminds us that God has really become man, that he rejected nothing in our humanity except sin, that his real body born of Mary rose from the dead, that his holy mother is now with him in soul *and body*. All this allows us to conjecture that the Beatific Vision establishes and nourishes our *human* joys with respect to what is most real in them and to what Christ has consecrated and sanctified.

There is also the essential theological principle that grace does not destroy nature but perfects it, and it follows from this that the life of glory will not supersede the life of nature perfected by grace but will perfect it as well. Even here on earth, when we see certain "successes" of grace in its true marriage with nature, we have a foretaste of the happiness which God wants to pour into our Christian hearts: marriage and the birth of offspring, the peace of family life when it lies open to grace, the calm that lies over nature, and its beauties. And to all this we might add the peace in our poor hearts when they have been broken by suffering. There are deaths in which "one sees heaven opened" (Jn. 1.51).

Perhaps it is our special role to give contemporary society the witness of true Christian joy. We shall reject neither the leisure of our age, nor the beauty of the earth, nor even a certain amount of comfort, but we must make it clear that our hearts are not ensnared by these things. We shall be human, deeply human, but at the same time we shall be aware, and show by the authenticity of our lives, that our expectations transcend a simple humanism. We shall learn to let ourselves be caught up in the currents of earthly life, but still more in those of the kingdom of God. And at the same time, with the help of grace, we shall bear our Christian witness through serenity in suffering and patience in trials.

It is perhaps in this way that our contemporaries will sense that Christ is in the midst of a world at once so lovely and in so much anguish: God's response to their quest for happiness, Christ crucified and blessed, whose reign will never have an end.

13. Christ Crucified

"But we preach Christ crucified, a stumbling block to Jews and folly to Gentiles, but to those who are called, both Jews and Greeks, Christ the power of God and the wisdom of God" *(1 Co. 1.23–24).*

Men of all ages, and perhaps more particularly our own contemporaries, are animated by a stubborn, even fierce, will to be effectual—that is to get results, to achieve some lasting work. And indeed such a drive is noble and fruitful, so long as it remains subordinated to the wisdom in which all values are integrated. Let us try to paraphrase St. Paul on this point: "The educated [the Greeks] search for wisdom, the realists [the Jews] seek power. But, as for us, we preach Christ crucified, a scandal to the realists, a mockery for the educated, but to those who are called, it is Christ the Wisdom of God and the Power of God." What a paradox! Or, rather, what a work of grace! Those whom God calls perceive in a mysterious way that God's manner of achieving his effects is of a wholly different order from the world's; it belongs to the order of his love, his Love who carried the cross.

A fact and a mystery

It has pleased God to save the world through the cross. Our faith must accept this statement as a statement of fact, with all the substantiality of a fact. The same thing holds true for all the essential points of revelation. God does not, first of all, speak to us in the sphere of speculation, but through tremendous actions with infinite implications, arising from his freedom and his love. Each time we say: It pleased God. It pleased God to be made man, and first a child; it pleased him to institute the Eucharist; it pleased him to be raised on the cross; it pleased him—and this sums up, and in a sense explains, everything—to love us.

Thus whenever our minds are called upon to accept the truth of an event which has the solid and existential character of fact and is at the same time a mystery of incalculable implications, since it was brought about by God, it is an occasion for him to reveal his wisdom to us.[1]

Such must be our first reaction in face of Christ's cross: to open ourselves to it as the major fact which stands out from the gospel evidence.

Jesus suffered to establish the kingdom of God. These are the few words, simple but with an extraordinary weight of meaning, which we must "ponder in our hearts." And if we want to carry on Jesus' work, we must be associated with his trials. Whoever we are, laymen or priests, this is the fundamental law of our baptism.[2]

Thus, the things we hate most—which, alas, are found everywhere—namely, suffering and death, are the things

[1] All Christian thought proceeds in this way. First it assembles, with reverence and faith, the data concerning God and the data concerning Christ (which present themselves to the eyes of our reason with their various proofs). From these data it elaborates a wisdom which strives to reconcile the orders of nature and grace and to manifest their hidden harmonies.

[2] Col. 1.24: "In my flesh I complete what is lacking in Christ's affliction for the sake of his body, that is, the church."

Christ chose in order to save the world. So true is this that we can no longer separate our Lord from his cross, his "faithful cross" which he espoused. Yet this cross is haloed with glory, because on the third day he rose from the dead. Can we utter a few stammering words about the wisdom and power of God contained in this event and in the mystery of the cross?

In our midst and in us

Let us say at once, with St. Paul, that this wisdom will not enable us to penetrate to the meaning of "what no eye has seen, nor ear heard, nor the heart of man conceived, what God has prepared for those who love him."[3] This is to say that the wisdom of the cross surpasses human comprehension, that it is sometimes cruelly disconcerting, and that nevertheless we shall hymn it eternally.

However, even here on earth we are able to say something about it, and here is a consideration we might start with: God, in order to save us, did not go in search of things which belong to the prerogatives of a few—wealth or knowledge; on the contrary, he accepted and in fact chose what every man carries with him—his suffering and death. By the same token, he was not content with addressing himself to our idealism, through speech; he personally took upon himself the things which affect our very being and substance—that is, our human suffering and death. Thus it is through what is at once most common, most intimate and most dreaded that he redeemed the world and continues to redeem it. And so the road of the redemption passes through the most poignant area of our human condition. Who can say now that Christ is far from

[3] 1 Co. 2.9, an allusion to Is. 64.4.

us, that he is a stranger? He enters and makes his way in us through what is, willy–nilly, a part of ourselves.

We talk about our technological success and the efficiency of our production, and there is nothing wrong in this. These things can glorify God. It may be our role, more than that of any other generation, to "baptize" these accomplishments and make them contribute to the building up of God's kingdom. But despite all this we must, until the end of time, reflect upon the fact that Christ, God made man, chose another way. He went directly into the thick of the fight—our suffering and death—and made this the road of our redemption.

Besides, it is not enough to suffer and die, and nothing more, in order to meet God. Of themselves, we know, suffering and death are only the bitter fruit of sin; they are part of a world—our world, the only one we know—tragically perverted by sin and enveloped with darkness. But from the heart of darkness sprang light. God-made-man, the Christ of the gospels, came into our world and took on our condition in all except sin. The Father did not make a special world for his convenience. God-made-man silently took his place in this world as it is, constantly wounded by sin and constantly healed by grace. He received what this world gives when it is under the influence of the Evil One; fell prey to the jealousy of religious leaders, the fickleness of the crowd, the treason of one friend and the denial of another, a trial and an iniquitous condemnation, the kind of capital punishment customary at the time—death, and death on a cross. There is nothing extraordinary in all this. The whole thing is human—really, sadly human.[4]

[4] In his beautiful book *The Cross and the Christian* (Herder, 1954), Father Régamey makes a very perceptive distinction between the raw

But what surpasses anything human is the peace coming down to us from this cross as we slowly turn the pages of the gospels in which Christ's passion is described to us. His words on this cross are words of peace rising out of human anguish and abandonment to the Father, and the most striking thing is the inexplicable certitude of the Crucified. And as we read on in the gospels, there is the empty tomb, there is the gospel story continuing simply, as if the jaws of death had never opened; there is Mary Magdalene recognizing her Lord; there is Peter having the whole flock entrusted to him as if he had never denied his Master; there are the acts of the apostles and Saul's conversion; there is the irresistible advance of the message of Easter throughout the world: there is our faith.

If the redemption is to reach us through our suffering and death, we must learn somehow or other to relate them to Christ, who takes them upon himself and makes them meaningful. For a living faith this relation to Christ is conscious; it is effected through a yes said to God in the hidden depths of our hearts which is often confused and painful. With many this assent remains only implicit. But God "tries the minds and hearts" (Ps. 7.9). He sees beneath appearances. Every man, the unbeliever included, is visited by God and judged

---

wood of the cross and the Holy Cross, mystery of salvation. The raw wood—that which causes pain—is always, in one way or another, provided by the world, inasmuch as it is a sinful world. Not God but the world itself is its immediate cause. But the power of grace suffices to transform it into a holy cross through the submission it effects in our hearts. Our sinful human condition can then be reversed and, transforming the fruit of sin into an instrument of salvation, we can sing: "In the midst of death we are in life." Thus the antiphon for Lenten Compline is turned around: *Media vita in morte sumus*— "In the midst of life we are in death."

or saved by him in accordance with the way in which he receives suffering and death.

This may be our first consideration in formulating the wisdom of the cross: in order to redeem us, God has taken the most ordinary, the most concrete, human things we have— things which the world, in love with its own efficiency, readily looks upon as waste and loss—things which the Christian, on the contrary, since Christ's passion, sees as sacred and invested with supreme efficaciousness: suffering and death accepted with faith and love.

In weakness, accepted and chosen

St. Paul casts another great ray of light on this mystery. He says, in substance, that for our salvation God chose the way of nothingness to bring to naught the things which are; of weakness to shame the strong. In the profound and moving style which is typical of him, the Apostle sets in striking contrast God's ways and man's demonstrations of power and pride.[5]

His teaching on this point sums up the eternal lesson given throughout Sacred Scripture: God gives his grace to the humble and resists the proud. Is it a question of delivering his people from Egypt? He makes use of a man who is helpless in the human sense. Against the Philistine giant, proud of his strength, he sends the child David. To his faithless people he sends Jeremiah, who can only stammer his message. And when the fullness of time has come, he gives men a sign which seems

[5] See, in First Corinthians, the whole first chapter and the second up to verse 6. See also what is called the hymn to the kenosis, or "self-emptying," of Christ out of obedience and love (Ph. 2.6–11).

absurd: "a babe wrapped in swaddling clothes and lying in a manger" (Lk. 2.12). Thus, it seems, the divine power adopts a pedagogy which consists in enveloping itself in weakness, so that the strong do not recognize him; but the humble of heart, on the contrary, exult with joy in adoring him.[6]

This does not mean that God does not know how to stimulate human success. This is no occasion for a systematic distinction between nature and grace. We can say, with Teilhard de Chardin, that the world's success is not indifferent to the kingdom of God. But one can easily see where uncertainty may come in: it is a question of knowing what end we are working towards and what practical means we are relying on. If it is solely a work of arrogant strength that we are pursuing and if the means of action depend on human forces alone, then we are engaged in nothing but a human undertaking and it is not at all certain that we are cooperating with God's kingdom. When some work for him is concerned, God, to remove all doubt, generally chooses instruments destitute of human power. Hence the striking disproportion between these instruments and the work accomplished: twelve ordinary men and the evangelization of the world; in our time Bernadette and the crowds at Lourdes, Thérèse of Lisieux and the missions of the whole world.

And when the work of God par excellence is concerned—the redemption of the world—God takes the poorest means possible, the most ridiculously futile: death on the cross. But make no mistake about it: He who is on the cross is, at this moment, Christ, the Power of God. God's power cloaks itself in weakness, but its advance in men's hearts and in history is

---

[6] This is the whole sense of the Magnificat.

irresistible: Christ Crucified, Wisdom of God, Power of God.[7]

We know all this in theory, but each time Christ's cross comes down on us we experience the same heartbreak, the same bewilderment, the same difficulty in believing. We need to have a real conversion in this regard, a radical reversal. Christ must teach us little by little, from within, his own truth —that is, that the real secret of power and effectiveness is to work with him, to rely on him more than on ourselves, to suffer with him: "My grace is sufficient for you, for my power is made perfect in weakness."[8] "In you, O Lord, have I hoped, I shall not be confounded forever."[9]

In the power of love

But the last word of the wisdom of the cross is given to us by St. John. He begins his narration of the passion with these words: "Having loved his own who were in the world, Jesus loved them to the end" (Jn. 13.1).

Even on this earth we are already well aware that the greatest source of power, the most lasting and at the same time the most hidden, is love. When love is real its usual accompaniments are self-forgetfulness and silence. Many are the homes established on the love of a mother and father. Love to the

[7] The whole of St. Paul could be quoted. See, among other places, 1 Co. 1.17–31; 2 Co. 4.7–18; 6.4–10; 12.7–10. We are not Christians until these great texts have, so to speak, become our flesh and blood.

[8] 2 Co. 12.9. Note that the Greek text brings together two most completely opposed terms: the power of God (*dunamis*) and the weakness of man (*astheneia*). The passage from one to the other occurs when man in his weakness relies fearlessly and with a profound certitude on the power of God.

[9] *Te Deum* (last verse).

point of self-renunciation constitutes the very fabric of human
life.

God-made-man has chosen this wisdom of love, but on his
own plane, having no dimension in common with ours. With
St. John we make bold to declare: "So we know and believe
the love God has for us."[10] But we are well aware that the
love which is in God, the love which is God, is a sacred
mystery which we can only adore. He is a mystery of love,
and thus we can rest assured that revelation of him face to face
will satisfy us beyond all our expectations. But he is also a
mystery guided by a wisdom which is not ours, one which
often baffles and sometimes crucifies us. And yet there are the
words of St. John; through the cross Christ "loved us to the
end." We must believe him and adore the cross as a mystery
of love. But that is a matter for faith.

Experience, indeed, teaches us that we need great grace if
the cross is to become a mystery of love in us. This should be
its normal effect: to open up deeper and deeper sources of
strength within us. Often, however, since we are poor creatures at best, suffering, when it goes on and on, seems to
exhaust our resources. All those who have been close to the
chronically ill, the severely handicapped, know this very well.
God's grace is especially necessary to us when we suffer.

This grace is offered to us. It flows constantly from the
cross on which God loved us to the end. Where is the source
of maximum effectiveness for the Christian? It is in the love
of Christ, which overcomes all suffering and all evil; it is also
in our own weakness and in our suffering united to Christ's.

[10] Among the last words Paul Valéry wrote in his *Carnets intimes*
were that the word love has been associated with God's name only
since Christ.

Of course it is our duty to meet precise and rigorous standards as to skill, to be in the first row, if possible, of those who work "efficiently." But we must constantly ask, "To what end?" and constantly keep our gaze on the way chosen by God-made-man. The supreme accomplishment is that of all-powerful Love on a cross.

14. O Death, Where Is Thy Victory?

"Death is swallowed up in victory. O death, where is thy victory? O death, where is thy sting? The sting of death is sin. . . . But thanks be to God, who gives us the victory through our Lord Jesus Christ" (1 Co. 15.54-57).

Such is the triumphal hymn St. Paul sings at the end of Chapter 15 of his first letter to the Corinthians, entirely devoted to Christ's resurrection and our own. And yet the same St. Paul utters these tragic words: "Sin came into the world . . . and death through sin . . . and so death spread to all" (Rm. 5.12-14). O bitter human destiny in which sooner or later death has the last word! But no, it no longer has the last word; it is no longer victorious, this death which has every appearance still of reigning over our great cities, our countrysides, our households. What has happened? On the road to Damascus St. Paul saw the glorified Christ and heard his voice. And he grasped the fact that Christ was living, that Jesus' disciples were right, that Jesus was truly risen from the dead. Everything, then, was changed for him. God loved us to this extreme: then who shall separate us from his love? (Rm. 8.35-39). Oh, extraordinary Christian destiny: to die with Christ and to rise with him!

In the midst of death . . .

One day or another we shall meet death. Although it is a certainty for all of us, we have not yet seen it for what it is. And then, suddenly, we meet it face to face: see it in the eyes of a friend, or the one we love most; sense its approach in ourselves. We have seen it inexorably at work, coming a little closer each day, and we have been helpless in our anguish.

Then, if we were believers, we prayed fervently. We were aware that we had reached a point of no return: now our faith in Christ was being put to the test. Death close at hand, death experienced, forced us to make a radical act of faith capable of reversing everything. And to what did this act of faith have reference? To precisely this, although still in obscurity: "My Lord, I believe that at a certain moment of human time your Son, Christ, truly rose from the dead, and that we shall rise in him because you are the God not of the dead but of the living."

We thus unconsciously gave expression to our faith in its most vital essence. No doubt you are aware that this used to be the very first profession of faith on the part of the neophyte when he was baptized: "If you confess with your lips that Jesus is Lord [the glorious title reserved for the one living God] and believe in your heart that God raised him from the dead, you will be saved" (Rm. 10.9). Such also was the precise content of the very first apostolic preaching: "This Jesus . . . you crucified and killed . . . God raised up" (Ac. 2.22–24). It was even the absolute condition for being an apostle: "So one of the men who have accompanied us during all the time that the Lord Jesus went in and out among us, beginning from the baptism of John until the day when he was taken up from us—one of these men must become with us a witness to his resurrection" (Ac. 1.21–22). Thus, to adhere from the depths of our hearts to the imponderable fact of the resurrection of Christ is to live our faith in what is most specific and fundamental to it. We are then "saved" in the sense that through this act of faith God brings us out of the darkness into light, from death into life (Col. 1.13).

Note that by making this act of faith we are not trying to minimize the reality of Christ's death, which would mean evading the concrete reality of our death and of the evil in the world; on the contrary, we think about it constantly and constantly rely upon it. For what actual reality would Christ's resurrection have for us if we had not first of all grasped the fact that he had undergone the total experience of death? It is this realism, embracing at once the actual death of Christ and his actual resurrection, which is expressed in the very first article of faith drafted by St. Paul: "For I delivered to you as of first importance what I also received, that Christ died for our sins in accordance with the scriptures, that he was buried, that he was raised on the third day in accordance with the scriptures" (1 Co. 15.2–4).

This epitome evokes the gospel narrative precisely—poignant, beautiful. Christ was seen in plain reality, hanging on the cross; the soldier opened his side with a lance; "he who saw it has borne witness" (Jn. 19.35). They took his body down from the cross and laid it in a tomb (Jn. 19.38–42). The stone was rolled away. Death passed through there—real death, as we know it. Everything was over.

What remains for ever humanly inexplicable is that the gospel history nevertheless survived, that it even advanced with fresh, triumphant impetus from this tomb. For on the third day the tomb was found empty, and so convinced were the apostles of Jesus' death that the truth of the matter never crossed their minds—that is, that he might have risen from the dead. They thought, as we should have thought in like circumstances, that some human agency had been at work: someone had come during the night and taken his body away. It took all of Easter day for light to dawn in their minds: the stupendous news was true: Jesus was walking the earth again, risen from the dead, now living. The Church in her world-wide mission had come into being. But let us note that the shock of the resurrection was so shattering to the witnesses of Christ *because* they had lived through the crushing hours of Good Friday and Holy Saturday, those overwhelming hours which seem to set the seal on the tragic reality of the end.

For us the lesson remains. Do we wish to give the resurrection of Christ its full weight? Then let us not be afraid of weighing human death, all human deaths. For as real as our deaths are, the resurrection of Christ is real with an infinitely greater reality. Listen to the triumphant cry of St. Paul: "For this slight momentary affliction is preparing for us an eternal weight of glory beyond all comparison" (2 Co. 4.17). Does not this sound like an easy optimism—"beyond all comparison"? Yet it is the plain truth. The resurrection of Christ raises all our deaths, however grievous, into an eternal weight of glory beyond all comparison.

We are in life

The face of human life is, and should be, radically altered by this certitude. But it is not changed in one day or even in

a few years. A whole life is needed for the resurrection's seed
of glory slowly to transfigure our joys and successes, our
sorrows and our death.

First of all, the face of death. Before we become capable,
like St. Francis of Assisi, of praising our Lord "for our sister
bodily death" there must be a veritable transformation of all
that which is most instinctive in us. We recall, perhaps, that
Bergson wrote, towards the end of his great work *The Two
Sources of Morality and Religion,* that if we were quite certain of living on, we should be unable to put our minds on
anything else. Pleasure would be eclipsed by joy. The fact of
the matter is that it is infinitely more than a survival—even
an endless survival—which is assured to us by our faith. It is
eternal life—that is to say, life with God, which transfigures
human life out of all comparison. But this life is given to us
through Christ's resurrection. Even in this world, and precisely in the reality of our bodily death, the glory of this
resurrection blossoms. We are aware of it, it is already at
work in our sufferings themselves. It would not bloom if we
did not suffer, if we did not die with Christ. And even as we
learn to die with him, we should believe that his glorious
resurrection is germinating and bearing fruit in us. Oh, happy
Christian condition in which everything is capable of trans-
formaton in Christ!

And not only is the face of our death transformed; so also
is that of our life and our joy. Everything—absolutely everything—must be caught up in our Lord's resurrection, not to
be diminished but to be purified and elevated. The world's
aspirations, great enterprises, human solidarity and the great
struggles for justice—all those movements which are so strong
in our time and yet so much overcast by intellectual con-

fusion—it is the role of the Christian to assume responsibility for them with clearsightedness, courage and hope, in such a way that they can be caught up in Christ's resurrection. On this earth it is charity, not of the spurious kind, whose inconsistency and ambiguity causes it to be rejected with violence by so many of our contemporaries in the name of truth, but true charity, at once divine and human, patient and courageous—this is the charity which is the sign on this earth that resurrection has already begun. Wherever an ounce of charity is found, there is a victory of the resurrection and a seed of transfiguration. To live a risen life with Christ is to live a life more and more permeated by true charity.

Here on earth "faith, hope, love abide, these three; but the greatest of these is love" (1 Co. 13.13). And death is swallowed up in victory.

15. Reconciled with God through Christ

We are familiar with this scene from the gospels. Peter has just denied Christ for the third time. Then, the text of St. Luke somberly relates: "Immediately while he was still speaking, the cock crowed. And the Lord turned and looked at Peter." This look, in its sadness, sincerity and love, pierced Peter's soul and converted it. "And Peter remembered the word of the Lord, how he had said to him: 'Before the cock crows today, you will deny me three times.' And he went out and wept bitterly" (Lk. 22.60–62).

Our Lord had to take the first step; he had to turn and fix his gaze on Peter.[1] And in an instant Peter, in this look, became aware of his sin, the extent of his wickedness and the infinite mercy of his Saviour. It is in this way that Christ brings to the men of all times the revelation of God's forgiveness. Without Christ and a personal God, man is scarcely able to endure the awareness of his sin without taking refuge in unconsciousness or falling into despair. With Christ and the God whom he reveals, man is aware of his sin with deep sorrow, but also with peace and a salutary change of heart. He knows his own misery, but he casts it on God. God is a God who forgives! What a total deliverance!

[1] We say in theology that grace is always "prevenient"—that is, it runs before, and stimulates, the human act.

My sin is ever before me

Without a personal God, we were saying, without this God whom Jesus has made known to us, man has great difficulty in dealing with his consciousness of sin without seeking distraction in pleasures or falling into despair. For a long time, perhaps, he will drink of the torrent of sin. Pleasures, enthusiasm for life, freedom, various interests—he is caught up by all these things in turn, and gradually they enslave him. Averting his gaze from the wrongness of things (of which a dulled instinct nonetheless warns him), extremely practiced in blinding himself, he does these wrong things, absorbed as he is in the "good" he desires. And then life does its work: first, difficulties, disappointments, obstacles, trials, coming to him, perhaps, through a merciful dispensation of God. One day or another, unless he has deliberately organized his life around sleep, his eyes are opened. At length—often at night, in bed[2]—he begins to take account of his life. The wrong he has done—he sees it now. He—yes, he—is the one who did it; he is responsible for this innocent suffering, this cowardice, this lie. Now his life is beginning to decline. He cannot begin it all over again. Can a man, when he is old, enter again into his mother's womb (Jn. 3.4)?

He then, perhaps, begins to put the question of God to himself in a serious way. The evil he has done—Another, infinitely more clearsighted than he, sees it too. Nothing is hidden from his sight. He "tries the minds and hearts." He

[2] Cf. the plaint of the psalmist (Ps. 6.6–7). Night is at once the time of darkness during which the wicked go about their nefarious business and the time of God's visitation during which the just man is purified.

has power to reject a man without hope of appeal and cast him into hell. "If thou, O Lord, shouldst mark iniquities, Lord, who could stand?" (Ps. 130.3). Already a strange form, mysterious yet familiar, begins to loom before him: death. It seems to him that he has not yet lived, and here, already, is death. We shall have to render an account to God for the life he has given us. How shall we weigh in the balance?

The man perceives, then, that most of the principles according to which the world lives are false. Under God's gaze, what part of his life, his intentions, will stand? What has he done for all the unfortunate people in the world? How well he looked after himself—far too well! It would be too easy to appear before God "just like that." And now the false notions about God begin to collapse: God the refuge, God who gives our conscience reassurance, God with whom we can set ourselves right with a few ceremonies or gestures. None of this holds up in the hours of greater lucidity. But often the Evil One comes then too. It is his hour. It is not without reason that he is called the Accuser.[3] He is merciless in his accusations. As is his custom,[4] he makes use of the very words of God. It is all too clear that we have done no good whatsoever: "We have become like one who is unclean, and

___

[3] Rev. 12.10. The Evil One, or the Devil, is called in Scripture "the accuser of our brethren . . . who accuses them day and night before our God." By contrast, first of all Christ, and the Holy Spirit after Christ's departure, are both called "the Counsellor" (Jn. 14.16; cf. 1 Jn. 2.1). By these terms, borrowed from legal language, we are to understand that the Evil One seeks to prosecute all children of God so as to prevent their birth or their growth. The Holy Spirit, on the contrary, in a hidden manner takes up the defense of the child of God, God's creation, who is seeking to be born.

[4] Cf. Jesus' temptation in the wilderness: the Evil One begins with a quotation from Scripture, and Jesus replies victoriously with another quotation from Scripture. Cf. Lk. 4.9.

all our righteous deeds are like a polluted garment" (Is. 64.6); "All men are liars" (Ps. 116.11, Donay). We have no way of knowing whether we deserve love or hatred. It is, on the contrary, all too obvious that we have done nothing but wrong, and the necessary good we have omitted to do. And our life is finished, quite finished.

O Lord, deliver us from the demon of despair!

God is a forgiving God

It is then, if he is a Christian, that another light, little by little, begins to shine out in the man's heart and slowly to deliver him into the freedom of truth. This light comes not because he is a man but because God is God. The man thinks about Christ, about his words, about the gospels. His thinking takes on a new and extraordinary tone. He thinks, for instance, about the fifteenth chapter of St. Luke, about all the parables on "what was lost"—the lost sheep, the lost drachma, the lost child—all ending in the same tender and triumphant way: "Just so, I tell you, there is joy before the angels of God over one sinner who repents" (Lk. 15.10). He thinks of the Christian prayer par excellence, in which the whole essence of the soul's relationship with God is contained, the Our Father, and he repeats it slowly: "forgive us our trespasses as we forgive those who trespass against us." Thus, he will not enter the kingdom of God which Jesus preached if he does not adapt himself, little by little, to God's own ways of mercy and forgiveness. He thinks of Christ, the Holy One: "You are the Holy One of God" (Lk. 4.34), "Which of you convicts me of sin?" (Jn. 8.46); thinks of this same Christ, who forgave.

The woman to whom many sins were forgiven because she

loved much; Peter, on whom his Master looked, and he wept bitterly—all these living beings, flesh and bone like himself, bring him deliverance because they all bring him the same fundamental revelation of a God who loves ardently and to the end. God is a holy God, and he is at the same time a God who forgives.

Let yourselves be reconciled to God

Listen now to St. Paul: "God through Christ reconciled us to himself and gave us the ministry of reconciliation. . . . We are ambassadors for Christ. . . . We beseech you on behalf of Christ, be reconciled to God" (2 Co. 5.18–21).

The Christian contrition which Christ brought into the world does not mean a sterile introversion, the sifting of one's conscience for sins and a persistent, confused feeling of guilt; it is a profound turning of one's heart to God in which, rejecting evil in principle and all the evil in oneself, one opens oneself to infinite love; then, reconciled with God in Christ, one finds oneself likewise reconciled with oneself and one's fellow men.

Indeed such a change of heart presupposes a sense of guilt. To acknowledge one's guilt—that is, to admit that we have let evil come into our souls—is the first step towards deliverance, the first awakening from sleep, and perhaps from death. But Christian contrition adds something specifically new to the sense of guilt: far from leaving us on our own, it firmly orients us towards Another on whom all salvation depends: God, Christ. Man is no longer alone, the prisoner of sterile remorse. He is with Another who brings him at once an understanding of his malady and the source of his healing. Now let him cast himself on Christ with all his faith and all his remorse; let him stop trying to justify himself, and likewise stop bringing accusations against himself which are actually false. Then Christ will reconcile him with the whole truth, the truth concerning God and the truth concerning men, which has been placed in them by God himself.

Truth and freedom, then, are the gradually ripening fruits of Christian contrition. Pascal has Christ say that if we knew our sins we would lose heart, but that as they are in the process of being forgiven, he will tell us to look and see the sins for which we are forgiven. In order to lead us into all truth (Jn. 16.13), the Holy Spirit needs—if we may put it that way—to begin by convincing us of sin (Jn. 16.8). If we were not convinced, we would find it difficult not to be superficial and pharisaical. But since it is the Holy Spirit who convinces us of sin, he pours into our hearts a deep sorrow, certainly, but not discouragement or despair, but rather a vigorous determination and a supernatural hope. "I will rise and go to my Father" (Lk. 15.18). Men, my brothers, are waiting. Come, rise up and be doing. "Love covers a multitude of sins" (1 Pet. 4.8).

In our time when so many discordant voices are making themselves heard on the subject of sin and guilt, sometimes to deny their reality absolutely, sometimes to find concepts to substitute for them, we Christians must submit to long and careful instruction based on scenes from the gospels and on Christian tradition. Here, in Christ, we learn what sin and forgiveness are. And may we, animated by the Spirit which was in Jesus, testify before the world as to what Christ intended his followers to be: men with depth and sincerity of character, not in the least pharisaical, understanding human weakness without ever saying that wrong is right, needing forgiveness and knowing how to forgive—men who, in the midst of the world, believe in a redemption because they nourish themselves daily with Christ, the revealer of God's forgiveness and the creator of newness of heart.

16. Christ the Bond between Men

Caiphas, the high priest of that year, had "prophesied" that it was preferable that one man (Jesus) should die for the whole people, and St. John makes the connection forthwith: "and not for the [Jewish] nation only, but to gather into one the children of God who are scattered abroad" (Jn. 11.52). Beyond Israel, tragically dispersed by the violence marking its history, the sacred author saw the whole of humanity. He was thinking very specifically of the spiritual race of the "children of God," of the "men of good will," of those, scattered over the whole earth and in all times, who seek God; and he declared that it was God's intention to gather them together in Jesus.

In our days of ecumenism and universalism, days of confusion and syncretism as well, what purity and strength, what fullness and hope, is required of our faith, if we are to labor in Christ and with him to gather into unity the scattered children of God!

To those who are born neither of blood nor of flesh . . .

It is necessary that our faith and our hope should have a firm hold on one thing above all: the ground on which the gathering of men into unity in Christ is slowly taking place over the centuries and the energies through which it is being effected. Let us immediately make it clear that this is not the work of "flesh and blood" but one of God alone. And indeed this presents a terrible trial for our faith: when daily a multitude of signs indicate that it is flesh and blood—economics, class, national aspirations, and so on—which are the basis for human groups, we are asked to believe, even while we fully acknowledge the tremendous influence of these factors, that there is another source of unity, another power at work in the world bringing it into oneness: the grace of the living God.

And here two perils lie in wait for our faith—perils which have been preached against so often that we hesitate to do it again, and yet we must again and again be made aware of them. On the one hand, we can take refuge in an "intellectualism" which comes closer to a sterile idealism than to the Spirit of God; and on the other, we can let ourselves be caught up in the seduction of "flesh and blood" as if only they were real. What we call "adult" faith, so long in the attainment, is it not precisely this—a plain, straightforward faith which in practice believes more in God than in the world; which, out of love, is not afraid to work in the midst of the world with God?

Those who intend to join in Christ's struggle to gather into unity the scattered children of God should constantly have in mind these two things which faith requires, and this will be, moreover, the source of a purification daily renewed. On the one hand, they must say no to everything which seeks to establish flesh and blood as the only values, the exclusive building materials of human solidarity. On the other hand, they must embrace the realities of flesh and blood and believe,

with all the intrepidity of their faith, that it is possible for
God to be present in them. Such is the belief of men of faith
who in the midst of an unbelieving society retain their awareness that Christ is fashioning the world in the direction of
unity.

This means that, more and more, two closely complementary qualities seem to be required by our faith: purity, thanks
to which we discern the true God by comparison with idols
and God-substitutes, and a sovereign magnanimity whereby
we have no fear of plunging into the current of the world.
It is only to the extent that we have these qualities that we
can hope to contribute to the unity of the world in Christ.

. . . but of the Spirit of truth . . .

It is evident that in Sacred Scripture the unity of mankind
rests, in the first place, on a certain divine revelation and, as
an immediate consequence, on the specific nature of the relationships of men to one another. Christ, the revealer of God,
gathers the scattered children of God into unity by enlightening their minds in their innermost depths through the same
divine revelation which he brought to earth. As soon as we
have established communication with a man which is in any
way personal, we begin to ask ourselves this fundamental
question: "Does he believe in God? And if so, what is his God
like?" This is a question bringing an answer which may fill
us with deep joy—we meet each other like brothers—or painful surprise—what is there in common between this man and
ourselves?

We know by faith that the divine revelation of our Lord
Jesus Christ is the only divine revelation in which the children

of God dispersed over the earth can fully recognize each other
and come together. But how shall this be done? We must
unite with a great integrity of faith an extraordinary gift of
tongues, capable of making known what is already the secret
aspiration of the human heart. This is an undertaking which
each Christian generation must carry out, but in our own it
is more urgent and more difficult. How are we to phrase this
revelation concerning God, the Father of our Lord Jesus
Christ, so that men of good will may recognize him and thus
gather together?

Most assuredly it will be necessary to set in relief the purest
and simplest features of God the Father, and this will mean
careful study on our part of the teaching of the apostles as
well as a real prayer life and much love. To be more specific,
let us say that the two fundamental characteristics of this God
of Christian revelation seem to be these: first there is the
reality of a God who is personal and transcendent; second
there is the reality of a God who is incarnate. It is in this God
alone, the only true God, that the scattered children of God
can be brought into unity; and this we believe with all our
hearts. We shall have had to pray a lot, think a lot, suffer a
lot, before this twofold image of the true God is inscribed in
our inmost being. This is not a matter only of book knowledge; it is acquired through the intercourse of a whole life
with God in which we are nourished by Sacred Scripture
and the Church.

It is from this living God that we may hope to learn to
grasp the various forms which the hope for God or the rejection of God may take among our contemporaries. If through
God's grace they are one day able to say, from the bottom of
their hearts, the "Our Father" which Christ taught us, then

they will, on this day, be close to us, truly our brothers, and we shall communicate with them in the same living and intimate knowledge of God. It is thus that Christ gathers us to him in the first place: through the knowledge of the true God which he pours into our hearts.

As a consequence of this our relationships with our fellow men will have certain notes: truth, simplicity, love, unselfishness, forgiveness, and so on. In this—in this especially, in one sense—is manifested the presence of the true God and the gathering together of men of good will. It is in this way that the children of God dispersed in the world discover the evidences of the true God, and it is, again, Christ who, through the new teaching of brotherly love, brings this gathering about.

. . . *and of the Spirit of love*

But it is the Holy Spirit of love alone who makes it possible for us to "live Christ"; purely intellectual faith is powerless to make this mystery real to us. If Christ is to become in very fact the bond between men, he must dwell in our hearts through a living faith; he must have become a reality for us, mysterious indeed but infinitely real—more real, in a sense, than even the realities of flesh and blood. It is only under this condition that the expressions "to live in Christ," "to love one another in Christ," have a meaning, the meaning of a new reality. It is only under this condition that Christ really gathers us together and is the bond between us.

Two examples will suggest more to us than a long talk:

During the Second World War the Germans arrested four Dominican priests at the Convent of St. James in Paris. At the prison, one of the German guards was a genuine Christian. The priests, who are still living, can bear witness to what this man was for them: strong, sensitive, loyal. They can testify that despite everything which separated them from him on the human level, Christ was the bond between him and them. For they all shared a life in Christ: the same faith, the same prayer, the same Eucharist. Surely one could cite a hundred cases in which Christ, the bond between men, fell under the blows of flesh and blood. But we can likewise cite a great number in which this bond held firm, precisely to the extent that the Christ life was lived.

Here is another example. A priest had had the joy of being the instrument of one of his fellow men's reconciliation with Christ. Thereafter they were intimate friends. On his death-bed this man grasped the priest's hand and said to him in a tone he will never forget: "My brother, my real brother in Jesus Christ." They had both learned by experience what an extraordinary weight of reality, both human and divine, is contained in this phrase: in Jesus Christ. Their kinship in Jesus Christ was not of the order of flesh and blood, and yet how totally real it was, with a reality which death itself could not destroy; for it was the work of Christ, safe in his hands. Let us simply think of the various realities of human life— home, friendship, profession, even politics—and we shall grasp the extraordinary change, especially in depth, which this new existence will effect in them—this life in Jesus Christ if it is really lived. It is thus that Christ really and concretely gathers together into unity the scattered children of God.

St. John explicitly mentions the redemptive death of Jesus as a necessary and decisive factor in human unity. For Chris-tian revelation sin is the radical cause of the dispersal of mankind, and sin has been conquered only by Christ's death on the cross. When certain evils break out in the world, there is no effective remedy for them except the total, silent sacrifice of certain lives. The law is eternal. If the work of Christ in drawing men into unity is to go on, there must be a large-minded and courageous expenditure of Christian thought. Human society must be built up through the efforts of a love full of hope. Finally, our lives must be offered. All the architects of peace are aware of this, but they are likewise aware, to their joy, that at every moment of human time a mysterious gathering is taking place, that of the scattered children of God brought back into unity through and in Christ, the bond between men.

Part III
LIKE EVANGELICAL MEN

17. A Sense of the Father

Gospel spirituality is nothing other than a Christian life
with the special flavor of its source, a most manifest trans-
parency to the gospel in its letter and spirit. It is this flavor
of the source, this deep fidelity to the word of Jesus as it
echoes in Scripture, which our contemporaries imperiously
demand from us. But viewed from outside or by those who
are only beginning to live by it, the divine simplicity of the
gospel takes on vast complications. Only gradually does one
discover the key idea which, once found, simplifies its spirit
most wonderfully. May we be forgiven for recalling here
what has been said by so many masters of the spiritual life?
A sense of the Father in heaven, of his kingdom on earth—
it is this which constitutes the spirit animating the Gospel
Christian and enables him to accomplish "impossible" things.

Our Father who is in heaven

It has often been noted that the radical difference between
the Christian and pagan mentality consists in the transition
from a universe dominated by necessity or fate to a universe
indwelt and governed by the one whom Jesus has made
known to us as his Father and ours. A sense of the Father:
it is this which transforms a soul in its innermost depths, and
theology, with characteristic precision, tells us that two fun-

damental "divine instincts" animate the supernaturalized Christian soul: the sense of God (the gift of fear) and the sense of the Father (the gift of filial piety). Recall to your minds the first three Beatitudes; they flow from this twofold instinct. The poor of the gospels, the meek, those who mourn: it is these in whom the spirit of God who is our Father lives and breathes.

We Christians call our God "holy." More than a moral category is involved here; the word refers to an order of being reserved to God. He is holy; that is to say, his Name is above any other name; he dwells in inaccessible light (1 Tm. 6.16); he is in an order proper to himself, infinite, sacred. Moses takes off his shoes (Ex. 3.1–6), and Peter falls to his knees, saying, "Depart from me, for I am a sinful man, O Lord" (Lk. 5.8). The Christian learns to live on terms of tender familiarity with God, and this is the mainspring of his joy, but his intimacy is always tempered by an immense reverence. Every day in the Preface of the Mass the Church has us recite the sacred Trisagion. Having united herself with the angels and the blessed in heaven, who see face to face the One whom no one can look upon and still live (Ex. 33.20), she continues:

We pray thee let our voices blend with theirs as we humbly praise thee, singing:
> "Holy, holy, holy Lord God of hosts;
> Heaven and earth are filled with thy glory."

This holy God, the infinite, the only God, our Lord calls "Father." And indeed he is the Father, both in the absolute sense, as the transcendent origin of all life, and in the sense that he is a person who cares for us, loves us. From a study of New Testament terms the fact emerges that for the early Christians "God" was "the Father." By calling him Father they entered into the secret of his love.

Our Lord, through his life and words, taught us to see everything in the light of this tremendous truth. Most assuredly he is aware of the extent to which we can be overwhelmed by distressing problems—earning a living, the illness of our loved ones, the burden of human suffering and social injustice—but all this, so wholly real in itself, he teaches us to see, not in a vacuum, but transfigured by the presence of his Father. Listen to him:

> Our Father who art in heaven,
> Hallowed be thy name.
> Thy kingdom come,
> Thy will be done,
>   On earth as it is in heaven.

This earth does not represent the whole of reality. There is the divine order. There is the Father, our Father, whom our Christian hearts have learned to name.

Fear not, little flock

For this Father who is holy is also our father. He has always revealed himself as at once transcendent and close. Where shall we seek him? Where shall we find him? Not at the *end* of something—the universe, our reasonings, our efforts—but at the *root* of everything, above all of our own hearts, which he created and indwells. Where is God? He is near, infinitely nearer than we can conceive. Love him, with the help of his grace, and we shall know where he is.

The disciple of Christ learns, little by little, to trust God, this Father, completely. He is neither a visionary nor an "innocent." Life has taught him what the world is like; he has experienced its cruelties as well as its beauties. Our God is often a hidden God: "My God, my God, why hast thou forsaken me?" (Ps. 22.1; Mt. 27.46). Yet, in the depths of his heart, a sound supernatural instinct impels him to say to himself: "Don't be afraid; abandon yourself and take up the struggle again quietly." "Abandon yourself"—this expression often scandalizes unbelievers. Aren't these words too easy to say? Doesn't this idea of "abandonment" serve as a pretext for all abdications? And this would be true if it were not into the hands of God that we abandon ourselves. It is not a question of abandoning ourselves to just anyone. We abandon ourselves to God, not to rest passively in his hands but to resume our struggle with him.

The experience of the saints teaches us how simplifying this sense of the Father is to the spiritual life when one really lives according to it. It is difficult, indeed impossible, to live according to the gospel if we begin by setting forth, with a kind of military precision, all its demands: to renounce oneself, to sell all one has and give to the poor, to take the words of the gospels to heart, and so on. There is truth in all this, far more truth than we are able to grasp, but taken en masse it would be overwhelming if our heavenly Father did not illuminate it by his presence. Take St. Francis of Assisi, for example; take Father de Foucauld; take all of those whom our Christian people, with a sure instinct, have called "evangelicals": they have all entrusted themselves to God without reserve. It is thus that they "lost themselves," almost unconsciously. Here we have the "key idea" of which they never let go, even in the midst of the severest adversities. Here we have the secret of their often heroic simplicity.

It is this response of abandonment which our Lord seems to have wanted to cultivate especially in the souls of his disciples. When he sends them out with "no bread, no bag, no money in their belts" (Mk. 6.8), it is to have them learn by experience that God would not let them down. "When I sent you out with no purse or bag or sandals, did you lack anything?" They said, "Nothing" (Lk. 22.35). Glory is given to God not by our lacking material means but by our reliance on him incomparably more than on material means. It is then that the "impossible" things become possible. Let us ask God for the grace to learn how to get out of our depth in him. And we shall be astonished to discover in ourselves the freedom of simplicity.

Seek first his kingdom and his righteousness

We shall find out that such an attitude is the direct opposite of laziness or indifference to worldly things. Doubtless a badly understood faith sometimes leads to a lack of any real interest in human effort. It is possible for us to become less courageous, less committed, than non-Christians to the struggles for mankind's temporal salvation. This is not the fault of our faith itself, it is the fault of our own faintheartedness. Moreover, the perfect realization in us of the unity of the gospel takes a long time. It seems as if God needed to take us out of the world, at first, in order to plunge us back into it later on.

He must first detach us from the world, and from the spirit of the world, so that he may teach us, little by little, what his kingdom is. His kingdom is not of this world. Essentially it is, in the last analysis, neither social nor political nor cultural. It is *religious*. The kingdom is a mystery in the strict sense of the word, one which transcends all social and political forms and hence is capable of assuming them all and transforming them from within. Owing to his lack of prayer and contemplative thought, the superficial Christian has a constant tendency to reduce the kingdom of God on earth to a human enterprise. The apostles themselves were very slow to grasp the true nature of the kingdom, and our Lord had to lead them to it gradually: "The kingdom of God is not coming with signs to be observed; nor will they say, 'Lo, here it is!' or 'There!' for behold the kingdom of God is in the midst of you" (Lk. 17.20–21). We ourselves, for that matter, militantly engaged in Catholic Action—apostles, we might say: Didn't we think, in the beginning at least, that something would change through our efforts, that the kingdom of God would more or less come, that we were going to change the world? And then God purified us. He taught us that his kingdom was even lovelier than we had supposed, that it was not made with hands, that it was his own kingdom, the mystery of his grace creating newness of heart in the Holy Spirit. And we learned to believe in his grace and to rely on it more than on ourselves.

But as soon as God purifies us, he sends us out into the world. "Go to my brethren and say to them," he says to Mary of Magdala (Jn. 20.17). If he did not purify us, would we be leaven for his kingdom? If he did not put us into the mass, how should it be leavened? It is his kingdom that we must seek, above all and always; but, animated by invincible hope, it is this world as it is that we must try to reconcile with him.

To see everything in the light of the Father—life, death, successes, failures—to live in every event the kingdom of God which is to come; to dare to undertake everything, with the power of God—all this is the spirit of the gospels at its source, and here is the secret of its simplicity.

"Fear not, little flock, for it is your Father's good pleasure to give you the kingdom" (Lk. 12.32).

18. Fear Not, Little Flock

What is this little flock to whom it pleased the Father to give a kingdom? It reminds us at once of the "remnant" of which Isaiah spoke, those few faithful souls who were to see God's promises to Israel fulfilled at last. It is the little flock of "God's poor" to whom alone the kingdom belongs; if we wish to possess it, we have no choice but to become a part of this flock. So let us begin to allow the word to enter our hearts and, little by little, convert us: for this kind of conversion continues throughout our whole lifetime. "Blessed are the poor."

Where your treasure is . . .

Our Lord denounced solemnly, even violently, the terrible danger of riches coming finally to possess our hearts: "But woe to you that are rich, for you have received your consolation" (Lk. 6.24). It is no exaggeration to say that in the gospels money is seen as the greatest of the obstacles which keep souls from the kingdom: "The cares of the world and the delight in riches choke the word, and it proves unfruitful" (Mt. 13.22).

Why is this? It is not that wealth—the earth and all it contains—is bad in itself. There is no Manicheism in the gospels; neither money nor the flesh is to be despised, for everything

God made is good in itself. But there is in our hearts a terrible danger of our becoming too attached to the things of this world. Men tend to stick to their possessions as if they were glued to them, to subordinate everything to them, even themselves. When a man is in this state of mind, you might say that wealth has closed his heart against everything else: he has become incapable of recognizing the kingdom of God. And this is tragic. In the midst of this world the reign of God is coming, and here are men thinking seriously of everything else but him!

It is easy, then, to understand why Christ spoke with such force in condemning riches: he was trying to pierce the darkness of our minds, to shake us out of our false sense of peace. The kingdom of God is at stake. He says to us, "You are sleeping, and the kingdom of God is at hand"; "Provide yourselves with purses that do not grow old, with a treasure in the heavens that does not fail, where no thief approaches and no moth destroys! For where your treasure is, there will your heart be also" (Lk. 12.33). The terrible danger of riches, as we said, is that they close a man's heart, so that he no longer thinks of anything else. Then the gospel bears no fruit in him. The same terrible law holds for individuals, families, social groups. When Christians are caught—like the rest of the world —by love of riches, they become, alas, just like those others. Their conversation is like everyone else's; or, if they do try to speak of Christ, they can no longer do so with vigor and meaning: the salt has lost its savor. With what can it be made salt again?

Let us dare to cultivate a taste for the wealth of God— love, peace, joy, all the fruits of the Holy Spirit of which St. Paul speaks. Let us practice openhanded generosity, always ready to listen to the demands of the kingdom and of our brothers—then, without knowing how it has come about, we shall find that we are less attached to the things of the world, freer in spirit. "It has pleased the Father to give you a kingdom." It is the experience of the kind of wealth we find in the kingdom of God which frees us from the evil of attachment to the riches of this world.

Do not fear

The gospel not only frees us from that attachment to riches which encumbers our hearts, but also from our fears, which are so closely connected with it. Our search for riches is often inspired by fear, the dreadful fear that one day we shall find ourselves without even the money to buy our bread.

God, who taught us through his Son to ask him every day for the bread we need, understands our concern very well. He knows how precarious, sometimes miserable, our human condition is. Is it surprising, then, that we have such a great need to feel secure in every area of our lives? Let us say again, God understands this: doesn't he ask us to bring security to each other, to be channels of his providence? To provide secure shelter, security in daily work, security for the sick and the old, security—including emotional security—for children?

And yet, in spite of all that is being done in these ways, men still feel that their position is precarious, and they are still subject to fear. This is where Jesus' teaching comes in: he tells us repeatedly that we have a father in heaven; he even tells us to address this father as "Abba," which is a small child's word for "father." It might be said that our hearts are Christian when we feel so sure we are God's children that we do speak so to him, and this experience of living in the light of revelation is the only thing which can take our fear away. To be "poor" in the gospel sense is to have a confidence in God which is deep and even fearless. The father of a family wondering how he is going to pay a bill that is coming due, a mother who feels her strength failing, an apostle suffering cruelly from loneliness and indifference—all these are poor indeed; what is asked of them is that they should become poor in Christ, entrusting themselves, heroically it may be, to God. This is the faith Christ "marvelled at," and the quality we admire most in the saints. They are not afraid to undertake anything at all: they have been delivered from fear.

You gave me food

Evangelical poverty, then, is not faintheartedness or laziness. Neither is it just any kind of freedom. It does free our souls, but only so that they may be filled with love, especially love for the poor.

"Poor" is a word that must be delicately handled—who can bear to be called "poor"? But poverty is real enough! How many men lack shelter, dignity, freedom, health, love or any kind of security? We may look for the poor afar off, when really we might find them close at hand. It is our business to discover them: "Blessed is he who considers the poor" (Ps. 41.1).

Let us resolve, quite simply, to ask God continually to open our hearts to the poor, to help us to see them, and that we may have the courage to do for them all that he would like us to.

A heart for the poor—Christ's heart. We cannot be Christian without a heart which is like his to some degree. The only true God, the God who has revealed himself to us, has identified himself with those who suffer from basic human needs: "I was hungry. . . ." We must constantly defend our love for the poor against the harshness and indifference of the world about us. This is not a spiritual luxury, it is elementary Christianity.

Seeing clearly. Both our hearts and our intellects are concerned in this matter of clear sight: we have to *learn* to see clearly, it is an art we acquire by degrees.

The courage to fulfill our commitments. Each of us must discover what it is that God requires of him, taking into account his gifts, his responsibilities and his aptitudes. For one, acts of charity; for another, union work; political or social work for another. One is to use his talent for speaking or writing, another is to be hospitable to those less fortunate than he is. Not all of us can join a world organization to help the poor, but we must all keep in mind what their problems are in this twentieth century. Each must find his own way, a way suited to twentieth-century Christianity, to answer the urgent call of Christ.

Proclaim the kingdom

No one can be a missionary of the kingdom unless he is poor in a Christian sense. If his heart is encumbered with worldly goods and the cares they bring, how can it be free to meet all the opportunities God in his wisdom wants to entrust to him? If his heart is full of his own concerns, how can it be full of the kingdom? And if it is not, how can he be a sign of the kingdom? How can his words about Christ and the gospel be convincing if he is really perfectly satisfied with this world? This does not mean that a man must get rid of all his material possessions—after all, he may have a wife and children to support!—but it may mean that difficult decisions will be demanded of him and of his wife and children. It does not even mean that a Christian cannot be "rich," so long as he knows that he holds his riches in trust from God (Lk. 12.21). But in that case his conversion will have to be especially radical and deep.

To be poor in Christ's way means to be free from fear, not just in moments of exaltation, but in a deep habitual faith which makes us see clearly. Do not the experiences of Christian laymen who are active in working for God witness to this?

We must beware of unreal romanticism: real mystics are never afraid of solid commonsense. "What is needed must be done," as good people say.

Nevertheless, the Christian soul is always called to aim at greater heights, greater truth. "Follow me" is what our Lord still says to every Christian. There is a particular way of doing this for each of us. We must be quite realistic about this and, instead of taking refuge in dreams or otherwise trying to escape, discover what the real answer is for each of us, and we should not mind if it is only a humble one.

Let us be possessed by the kingdom: let us dare to abandon ourselves to the divine providence of the Father: let us be consumed by care for our brothers: this is the real and true way of being poor in the way of Jesus—and how happy we shall be!

19. The Full Grain in the Ear

Our Lord always asks us to look ahead, towards the inconceivable future God has prepared for those who love him. Thus we are not men on whom night is drawing in, but men living in expectation of dawn. "More than a watchman for the morning" we long for the coming of the Lord as "the radiant morning star." The road which leads to Christ is not behind us in the past but before us in the future. Even though we are not always conscious of it, our hearts are full of a deeply grounded hope, poured into them by the gospel. How are we to bring this hope to our contemporaries, so many of whom "have no hope and are without God in the world"; and to those who nowadays believe they have found, in the wreckage of Christian hope, a better hope, one entirely of this world?

The Lord who is to come

It is important that we should understand clearly what it is we hope for: the Lord who is to come and his kingdom which is always coming, and in another sense is already here. When the first Christians began to experience persecution, St. John, the beloved disciple, revived their courage by turning their minds to the Lord of Glory, whom he spoke of as: "He who is and who was and who is to come" (Rev. 1.4–8). This is the real object of Christian hope: God is to come to this earth, and his kingdom too is drawing near. It is in the light of this knowledge that we must use all our strength in working for him.

We know how long it took our Lord to make his apostles understand the exact nature of this "blessed hope." A real conversion was necessary for them, and so it is for us: a conversion in which a man, from being oriented towards the things of this world, gradually begins to see and turn towards that other kind of reality, only seen by those whose hearts are opening to God. How long it takes us really to come to believe in the kingdom of God on earth, to believe in it strongly enough for it to become our whole inspiration, the source from which we draw our enthusiasm and our patience! And yet, only this is true Christian hope.

Christ begins by gradually changing our vision of reality. Looking about the world, what do we see? Wheat growing for bread, houses built by men, factories; and, at another level, the joys of human hearts, and unfortunately their sufferings and rebellions too. All these things we must learn to see just as they are, but we must also learn to see beyond them to another kind of bread, another city, another joy, another suffering—the cross of Christ. What are we seeing then? The boundless kingdom of God, penetrating our world with love.

As he changes our way of looking at the world, he gives us something new to look forward to. We all hope for various small joys in this world, human joys by no means to be despised, and there are special, intimate expectations of joy—the anticipation of a mother expecting her child, for instance. But beyond all these natural expectations there is the super-

natural hope which stirs the people of God: Christ is coming;
his kingdom is always on the way!

Our Lord taught us that this kingdom is at once close at
hand, "in our midst," and yet is still to come. Its presence
among us is already a reality: "The kingdom of God is not
coming with signs to be observed, nor will they say, 'Lo,
here it is!' or 'There!' for behold, the kingdom of God is in
the midst of you." Often we go looking for it afar off, we
complain that it is impossible to see it, we are distressed because we cannot find it, forgetting that all the time it is close
to us—within reach of our hands and hearts! It is to be found
in our own joy, in any affectionate heart, in someone's sorrow,
in a vagrant—one of God's beloved poor who is passing by;
in these things and also in the great events of history. See
what simple words our Lord uses as images of his kingdom:
the seed growing in secret, the mustard seed which will become a tree, the leaven making the dough rise. All these images
tell us that the kingdom is already here, and at the same time
that it is not yet here in its fullness: the end is still to come.
That is why there is not only certitude in Christian life but a
tension as well. A certitude: God is here; so St. John of the
Cross can say: "Why do you wait, my soul, to love God in
your heart?" A tension: "When will you come to us, Lord;
when shall all know you?" And lastly, an invincible hope—
for you are coming, O my God, and nothing will be able to
prevent it.

And let us not be too quick to say to ourselves that we just
think like this in moments of exaltation or alienation from the
world. This hope of God's coming first stirred in the People
of the Promise, and through all the centuries since it has not
died; it is the life of the Church, springing up afresh in each

generation, witnessed to in every age by the countless men and women who through their lives, their joy and their suffering, attest that the kingdom of God is among us and that its fullness is indeed coming. And this is the essence of Christian dynamism.

The cross, the power of God

But paradoxically, it is usually through suffering and the cross that the kingdom comes. This was the way that Christ chose: "From that time on Jesus began to show his disciples that he must suffer many things . . . be killed, and on the third day be raised." It is through the cross still that it comes into each of our lives in this world. Do you remember what St. Paul calls the cross? Is it weakness? Folly? So men call it, he says, but it is in fact "the power of God." In every one of us there is a will to power: it is on this that the empires of the world are founded. But when God comes, his will is only to serve—as Christ did, whose service of us led him to become obedient even to death on the cross. It is in this strange way that God's power is shown, by a love stronger than evil.

St. Paul experienced this contradictory power even in his own body. Note the kind of antithesis which comes out in his style: "God's power is made perfect in weakness" (2 Co. 12.19). It is where human hope ends that our supernatural hope begins. Even for saints the cross remains the cross: suffering is not lessened, but it is transformed, and through it the kingdom of God continues to come.

"So we do not lose heart. Though our outer nature is wasting away, our inner nature is being renewed every day" (2 Co. 4.16).

Behold, I make all things new

Resurrection is not simply something to look forward to in the last days: Christ has already risen, and because of this the promise of resurrection is already transforming the world. This transformation begins in the depths of our hearts; then the hope of what is to come involves our bodies too. Our own bodies; but also, let us remember, those of our children. It is no small thing to bring children into the world; they too are destined to rise again to everlasting life. And finally we come to see that what our human hands have made, if it was in some sort done for God, will not be lost either. This world will pass away insofar as it is a world of sin and change, but insofar as it is already a resurrected world it will not pass. We should then, with God's grace helping us, labor so that even our human technical achievements may help to make this world truly God's world, already reconciled with him in Christ. Our real achievements on this earth are not a matter of indifference to the kingdom of God.

And I heard a great voice from the throne saying, "Behold, the dwelling of God is with men. He will dwell with them, and they shall be his people, and God himself will be with them; he will wipe away every tear from their eyes . . . for the former things have passed away" (Rev. 21.3–4).

The full grain in the ear

It is St. Mark who gives us the beautiful parable of the seed growing in secret (4.26.29), which is so full of hope—hope which is natural, but supernatural too. In it our Lord is showing us his Father's way of working, and how good it is. We can rely on the life in the seed and the nourishing earth to bring forth fruit. "So why," he asks us, "do you worry? As if you too were living without God and without hope!"

O Lord, give us living hope: even if it is as tiny as a mustard seed, it will give us new strength to work for you, because we shall know that you are indeed coming, and our brothers in the world will learn to believe it too.

20. As One Who Serves

The message of the gospel is a message of fundamental conversion, a complete reversal of our too human point of view, a turning to a higher wisdom which, if we accept it, enlightens everything: this wisdom is love. This conversion centers around a certain number of decisive points. Thus, the parable of the Pharisee and the publican (Lk. 18.9–14) teaches us to give up all our systems of self-justification and instead to rely upon God. Today, our Lord teaches us another principal point: the greatest in his kingdom is he who knows how to humble himself; the leader, he who serves (Mt. 18.4; Lk. 22.24–27). Let us listen with the attitude of a disciple who longs with all his heart to be taught by Christ.

But not so with you!

St. Luke shows us the scene at the last supper. Even then he tells us there was a dispute among the twelve about which of them was to be the greatest. And this after three years of living with our Lord! How deeply important to our wounded nature is the miserable desire for honor! And how clear it is that there must be a real change in us if grace is to succeed in moving and converting us on this point. But let us sit at our Lord's feet and listen to this gospel:

A dispute also arose among them, which of them was to be regarded as the greatest. And he said to them, "The kings of the Gentiles exercise lordship over them; and those in authority over them are called benefactors. But not so with you; rather let the greatest among you become as the youngest, and the leader as one who serves. For which is the greater, one who sits at table, or one who serves? Is it not the one who sits at table? But I am among you as one who serves" (Lk. 22.24–27).

You see how "the kings of the Gentiles lord it over them" is opposed to "but not so with you. . . ." This is a complete reversal of our usual way of behaving, something truly new: our natural behavior is to belong to another world. We must forget earthly values and enter into the ways of God. And here God-made-man is teaching us something truly amazing: among us *he* is the one who serves. We belong to his spirit only when our conversion on this point has begun.

Then his "but not so with you" works within our hearts with an authority which otherwise is humanly incomprehensible. We realize that this gospel teaches us no secondary point but something fundamental. Have we the mind of Christ, are we his disciples? To answer this question, let us ask ourselves what our basic spiritual attitudes are. Do we wish to dominate, or to serve, others? Do we wish to be called benefactors, or do we sincerely wish to be servants? We must realize that this amounts to two fundamentally different worlds.

He began to wash the disciples' feet

St. John tells us how the Lord took a servant's part: he washed his disciples' feet. Let us listen fervently to the gospel read on Holy Thursday:

Now before the feast of the Passover, when Jesus knew that his hour had come to depart out of this world to the Father, having loved his own who were in the world, he loved them to the end. And during supper, when the devil had already put it into the heart of Judas Iscariot, Simon's son, to betray him, Jesus, knowing that the Father had given all things into his hands, and that he had come from God and was going to God, rose from supper, laid aside his garments, and girded himself with a towel. Then he poured water into a basin, and began to wash the disciples' feet, and to wipe them with the towel with which he was girded (Jn. 13.1–5).

You must have noticed the contrast between the majesty of the beginning of this text and the simplicity with which it continues. The beginning is in St. John's formal manner, as when he begins his gospel with "In the beginning was the word." So here, he speaks of Jesus in his divine nature. After this, it is all the more startling to see our Lord behaving like a servant, doing what slaves did in those days. He lays aside his garments, girds himself with a towel, fills a basin with water, kneels in front of each disciple and washes his feet and dries them with the towel. St. John saw him do all this. He recounts our Lord's actions one by one. This is not legend: Jesus really did all this. Why? To open our eyes, to deliver us from the spirit of pride.

When he had washed their feet, and taken his garments, and resumed his place, he said to them, "Do you know what I have done to you? You call me Teacher and Lord; and you are right, for so I am. If I then, your Lord and Teacher, have washed your feet, you also ought to wash one another's feet. For I have given you an example, that you also should do as I have done to you" (Jn. 13.12–15).

"I have given you an example." Men need examples. When a man no longer sees his way clearly he becomes confused; but if, looking back, he can remember a helpful example, his doubts disappear: he sees the path ahead plainly again. Christ gave us Christians this example of humility to keep in the depths of our hearts: when we remember Christ washing the feet of his disciples, we see everything in its right order again.

St. Augustine writes: "Humility is so important for man that God in his greatness wanted to give him a perfect example; for man would have perished forever, victim of his pride, if God had not saved him through his humility" (*Com. in Jn.* 13.2–5). If we accept and follow this path shown to us by the Word made flesh, we shall find once more the road to paradise.[1]

We must admit that this example is difficult to follow. And yet it must play a part in our lives if we are to be true disciples, not "carried about with every wind of doctrine" but mature men (Ep. 4.14).

It is not a question of giving up the authority entrusted to us. This is not at all what Christ wants of us. On the contrary, he says: "You call me Master and Lord, and you are right, for so I am." Courageous acceptance of authority is an excellent way of serving; it is often the most crucifying way. We sin as much by refusing to exercise authority as by the abuse of authority.

Nor does this great doctrine mean an escape from life's

---

[1] This is the great theme of recapitulation, so dear to the Fathers. To save us, Christ took the opposite way to that which we followed (and still follow) to our loss. Instead of behaving like a king, he took the role of a servant. That is why we do not find Christ by exalting ourselves but by humbling ourselves, not by ruling but by serving. If we do this, we find we possess everything we thought we had lost. (Ph. 2.6–11 is St. Paul's great text on recapitulation.)

responsibilities. Let us honestly recognize that there have been
serious errors on this point in the past and will be in the
future. It is all too easy for certain natures to follow a path
which they wrongly suppose to be the path of service and
Christian unselfishness, when it is really a path of fear and
selfish hanging back. We must, on the contrary, rouse ourselves to high courage, even daring, in order to undertake
great things for God.

But what is even truer than we can imagine is the fact that
the example of Christ reaches down to the depth of our sin-
wounded souls, to uproot the old pride which imprisons us.
This is the crucial point on which our Christian conversion
is decided. Precisely here there is, or is not, a point of turning,
a passing from one world to another. We shall recognize the
truth of this not by words, but by living it. Let us try to do
so with grace: let us take the big step and become servants
with Christ, in his way. Then in all areas of our lives—family,
profession, even politics—we shall know that we have passed
from death to life and that we are free men, delivered from
the prison of pride. In order that we might learn to live the
new commandment of fraternal love we needed the practical
example given us by Christ. The Christian way of loving one
another is to become servants like Christ and with him.

21. The Experience of the Cross

On Good Friday the Church calls our attention three times to the cross of Christ in a progressive unveiling. Alas, three times are not too many if we are to see the whole cross plainly in our own lives! Let us not shrink from it, but listen to what our Lord teaches us about his cross.

He began to show them . . .

St. Matthew gives us the exact time when Christ unveiled the cross to his disciples, telling them what the future would bring. He had waited eighteen months. First he had to bind them to him with ties of faith and love. The cross is only bearable when it is borne with Jesus. Listen to the gospel:

From that time Jesus began to show his disciples that he must go to Jerusalem and suffer many things from the elders and chief priests and scribes, and be killed, and on the third day be raised. And Peter took him and began to rebuke him, saying, "God forbid, Lord! This shall never happen to you." But he turned and said to Peter, "Get behind me, Satan! You are a hindrance to me; for you are not on the side of God, but of men" (Mt. 16.21–23).[1]

[1] In addition to the veiled predictions (as in Mk. 14.8; 2.20; Lk. 12.31–35; Jn. 2.18–22), the gospels report three fully explicit predictions of the passion and the resurrection of the Lord. The first, after Peter's profession of faith (Mt. 16.21–23 and parallel passages of

Why did he call Peter Satan? Let us go back to the scene of the temptation in the desert (Mt. 4.1–11). The Messiah has two choices before him. The first is a worldly and easy messianism; the other, chosen for him by his Father, and predicted by Isaiah in the figure of the mysterious Servant of Yahweh (Is. 53). Satan, he who "scrambles God's plans," is there. He does not know whether Jesus is the Christ or not. But he is sure he will win Jesus if he can lead him on the path of ease, where stones change to bread, the marvellous abounds, and power is given over human kingdoms. And we know which path Christ chose; "Begone, Satan! For it is written, 'You shall worship the Lord your God and him only shall you serve.' " Now on the road to Caesaria Philippi, Peter, without meaning to, plays the Evil One's game. Facing the cross which Christ is unveiling before him, he cries: "God forbid, Lord! This shall never happen to you." Again Christ sees the two roads before him: the one prepared by his Father which leads to the cross (and beyond it, glory), and the other road which human nature so longs for: the road that does not lead to a cross. And with the same sureness, the same authority as he showed in the desert, we hear him say, "Get behind me, Satan! You are a hindrance to me.[2] For you are not on the side of God, but of men." O the mysterious, O the terrible, wisdom of God, who has chosen this way for his Son, that

---

Mk. and Lk.); the second, after the transfiguration (Mt. 17.22–23 and parallel passages); the third, at the time of the last journey to Jerusalem (Mt. 20.17–19).

[2] Scandal, in Greek *scandalon*, means stumbling block. Thus Peter, with his too human feelings, is, without knowing it, the stone against which the Evil One would like to see the Messiah stumble and be deflected from his course. St. Paul (1 Co. 1.23) uses the same image: "Christ crucified, a stumbling block to Jews."

he should save the world through suffering and a shameful death on a cross!

We can understand, then, that the disciples were afraid and did not dare question him (Mk. 9.32). St. Mark gives a striking account of the small group going up to Jerusalem for the last week.

And they were on the road, going up to Jerusalem, and Jesus was walking ahead of them; and they were amazed, and those who followed were afraid (Mk. 10.32).

But though Jesus unveils his cross more and more clearly, he never allows it to seem like a great chasm of death with nothing beyond it. He always shows that it opens onto life. On three different occasions the same short phrase recurs with the same triumphant ring: "And on the third day he will be raised" (Mt. 16.21; 17.23; 20.19).

O Lord, always give us enough faith so that we may never doubt that your resurrection already lights up our cross.

My hour has not yet come

Every man is born into this world for a certain hour which God has determined in his wisdom and which he alone knows. This hour is what gives meaning to a man's whole life, it is the time which can redeem and illuminate everything else. Christ tells us that his hour was the time of his passion, when he glorified God and God in return glorified him (Jn. 17.1).[3]

[3] St. John is especially fond of this mysterious expression, the "hour of Jesus." It always refers to his glorifying passion—that is, his passion accepted out of love, thus glorifying the Father and consummated by the Father in glory (cf. Jn. 2.4; 12.27–28; 13.1; 17.1).

This too he revealed, but only by degrees. At Cana, he said his hour had not yet come (Jn. 2.4). The Virgin did not understand this clearly yet. At this country wedding, fore-shadowing another much more solemn marriage, Mary prayed because there was no more wine. He granted her request, and St. John writes with awe of this first miracle: "He manifested his glory, and his disciples believed in him" (Jn. 2.11). When his hour does come, when the Son of God is united eternally with our poor humanity—in a word, on Calvary—he will speak to his mother, calling her by the same title "Woman," and he will give her a share in his hour.[4]

But standing by the Cross of Jesus were his mother, and his mother's sister, Mary the wife of Clopas, and Mary Magdalene. When Jesus saw his mother, and the disciple whom he loved standing near, he said to his mother: "Woman, behold, your son!" Then he said to the disciple, "Behold, your mother!" And from that hour the disciple took her to his own home (Jn. 19.25–27).

It was at this hour, the hour of Calvary, that Christ was glorified, because it was the climax of his obedience. There,

---

Our Lord spoke also of his "cup," the cup promised to those who dream of the places of honor in his kingdom (Mt. 20.20–23), the cup which his human nature fears (Mt. 26.39), the cup which his Father has given him and he will drink (Jn. 18.11). With this cup he also associates a "baptism" of suffering (Mk. 10.39; Lk. 12.50). These various expressions are poignant because they are a direct echo of Christ's words.

[4] Father Braun, in his beautiful book, *La Mère des Fidéles*, an essay on St. John's Marian theology, shows how the scenes at Cana and on Calvary throw light on each other. Thus he is faithful to the exegesis of the Fathers and shows that he understands St. John's way of writing. This is indeed no artificial comparison, but a very profound one.

in the mysterious wisdom of God, he transformed the bitter fruit of sin, our sufferings and death, into works of love and life. And he dreaded the ordeal: he went through agony.

"Now is my soul troubled. And what shall I say? 'Father, save me from this hour'? No, for this purpose I have come to this hour. Father, glorify thy name" (Jn. 12.27–28).

But "when Jesus knew that his hour had come to depart out of this world to the Father" (Jn. 13.1), he loved us to the end and was glorified. Listen to St. Paul:

. . . Christ Jesus who, though he was in the form of God, did not count equality with God a thing to be grasped, but emptied himself, taking the form of a servant, being born in the likeness of men. And being found in human form he humbled himself and became obedient unto death, even death on a cross. Therefore God has highly exalted him and bestowed on him the name which is above every name, that at the name of Jesus every knee should bow, in heaven and on earth and under the earth, and every tongue confess that Jesus Christ is Lord, to the glory of God the Father (Ph. 2.5–11).

Such is the hour of Jesus, that of his glorifying passion, which gives meaning to his whole life. We also have our "hour." Only God knows when it is. It is no use our worrying about it, but we must pray that we may be found faithful when it comes. If we are faithful, that hour will be the fulfillment of our lives, our final success. This is no trifling matter: it is our duty to prepare for it as well as we can. Whether we succeed or not is not a matter of indifference to the kingdom of God. It may not be our "hour" yet, that hour for which we were born, and which will determine our eternal destiny. But we know that it is at the hour of the cross that God weighs us and that we can either glorify him or refuse to. The Lord said to Peter: "When you are old, you will stretch out your hands, and another will gird you and carry you where you do not wish to go" (Jn. 21.18).

O Lord, grant that we may all glorify you by accepting our deaths out of love!

In a world which has faith only in material efficiency, in the salvation of men through science and technology, how strange seems our Christian faith in the salvation of the world through the cross! We even find ourselves almost doubting this redemption ourselves. Yet we only need to open our gospels, or to look at the crucifix on the wall in our home, and its truth shines out before our eyes and in our hearts. Or we can descend into the depths of our own hearts, our hearts that will stop beating one day, and recognize that we know death is making its way towards us. Then we see that suffering and death are the most profound, the most intimately personal, of human experiences. Why, then, should we wish God to be absent from them? And when we reread, slowly and lovingly, the simple and touching words in which eyewitnesses tell us what they saw and heard when Christ was on the cross, how close God seems to us then! "Father, forgive them, for they know not what they do. . . . Today you shall be with me in paradise. . . . My God, my God, why hast thou forsaken me? Father, into thy hands I commend my spirit."

And from the depth of our hearts, with God's grace, we believe that our sufferings and death are the beginning of the glory of our resurrection. This is the presence of Christ's cross in the world.

22. I Give You a New Commandment

Why should this commandment of fraternal love be called new? It is new, new as the union between God and ourselves brought about by Christ; new as our hearts at Easter, hearts reborn of water and the Holy Spirit. With our old hearts, worn away by sin, we could not truly love each other. This is the sense in which this commandment is new: only hearts reborn by his grace can understand and follow it. In the midst of a world where violence, hatred and love intermingle in such a confused manner, the supreme testimony of the gospel Christian is his belief in love.

You shall love your neighbor as yourself

We know the scribe's question:

"Which commandment is the first of all?" Jesus answered, "The first is, 'Hear, O Israel: The Lord our God, the Lord is one; and you shall love the Lord your God with all your heart, and with all your soul, and with all your mind, and with all your strength.' The second is this, 'You shall love your neighbor as yourself.' There is no other commandment greater than these."

And the scribe answered:

"You are right, Teacher; you have truly said that he is one,
and there is no other but he; and to love him with all the heart
. . . and to love one's neighbor as oneself, is much more than all
whole burnt offerings and sacrifices." Jesus said to him: "You are
not far from the kingdom of God" (Mk. 12.28–34).

Thus, the kingdom inaugurated by Christ does not require
animal sacrifice, it requires only love. To recognize this is the
first and fundamental conversion, and it must be continually
renewed. That we should practice a few observances, however
necessary they may be, is not enough; this would make our
religion little more than ritual. Something more is needed:
we must love.

Serene and unchangeable truth of the gospel! How slow
our hearts are to love, how easily scandalized! In the case of
some people we even feel revolted by the idea of loving them.

"You shall love your neighbor as yourself." Our Lord
quoted this commandment from the Old Law (Lv. 19.18).
God does not contradict himself. He restores and completes
what he had already established in the beginning (1 Jn. 2.7–
10).

As yourself. This does not mean with the same intensity,
or to the same extent, but with the same kind of love as that
with which you love yourself. And how do you love yourself?
With the kind of love one has for a person. Then you should
not love your neighbor as if he were a thing. Are you aware
that you have some dignity of your own—your own love,
your own sufferings? Then loving your neighbor must mean
being aware that all this is true of him too. You should listen
to what he has to say, as you like to be listened to, and to feel
that you are understood. Science has no bearing on this level
of knowledge: the intuition of love is needed. As you know

yourself to be in your own heart, try to understand and love your neighbor as he is in his heart. Otherwise you are not loving him as you love yourself.

The scribe, still worried, asked our Lord the great question which we will ask ourselves at some time: "Who is my neighbor?" My heart, he was thinking, is too small to love the whole world: I am only a man.

The ordinary meaning of "my neighbor" is someone close to me, someone to whom I am bound by natural ties; my family, especially my immediate family, or the people who live in the same apartment house with me, or in my neighborhood, people in the same milieu, who had the same kind of education I had—in fact, people of my own class, profession, race and religion. But there are so many other people in the world: what about them?

Natural ties are, of course, real. When they are established by God—as marriage is, for instance—they are sacred. There is an order in charity, and we know how very carefully St. Thomas tries to discern it (S.T., II-II, q. 25 and 26).

And yet how clearly the newness of the gospel shines forth here! The scribe asked, "Who is my neighbor?" Jesus returns to the problem: "It depends on you whether all men shall become your neighbors!" We know the parable. A wounded man is left beside the road. Who is going to be his neighbor? Not the priest or the levite, who pass by, but a Samaritan, one regarded as a schismatic, a foreigner. It is he—the schismatic, the foreigner—who stops, listens to the wounded man's groans, and sets him on his ass. "Which of these three," Christ asks, "do you think, proved neighbor to the man who fell among the robbers?" The scribe said: "The one who showed mercy to him." And Jesus said: "Go and do likewise (Lk. 10.36–37).

It is not, then, so much a question of who, in the material

sense, is my neighbor as of becoming, through love, the neighbor of my fellow man. The problem of the neighbor ceases to be primarily a question of physical proximity to become one of spiritual reality, of love. Without denying natural realities of friendship, the gospel brings about an extraordinary expansion of our hearts. I must approach any man through love, especially if he is wounded, and if I should have to go out of my way to avoid him.

As I loved you

Only with Christ has the newness of fraternal love been fully understood and lived. His love and his grace were necessary to effect this radical transformation in our hearts. That is why he tells us that fraternal love is a new commandment, his commandment, in which the whole spirit of his teaching is expressed. Its newness in relation to the old law lies in the fact that now it is *his* love with which we love. "Even as I have loved you . . . love one another" (Jn. 13.34). A new kind of love appeared on earth with Christ.

One recalls certain remarks of Bergson's in his *Two Sources of Morality and Religion*, to the effect that since family, fatherland, and humanity seem to be ranged like ever widening circles, one might expect that the love of humanity would come to us as naturally as the love of fatherland and family; whereas the truth of the matter is that the family and the social group are the only ones having a foundation in natural instinct, and the social instincts actually lead to conflicts between societies rather than contributing to the unity of humanity. The mystical love of humanity is something quite other, for it coincides with the love of God for his handiwork and contains the secret of Creation.

Coincides with the love of God.... Christ says to us, with divine simplicity: "Even as I have loved . . . love one another." But if we are to love as he loved us, a merely moral effort will not avail, for loving as he loved, coinciding with the love of God, is to love creatively, and for this we must be born again through the Holy Spirit.

Our whole lives are given us so that we may grow daily a little more in this love in which we are new creatures in Christ, this love which is beyond the powers of any man's nature. This growth is perhaps especially difficult for the lay person, faced with the ruthless struggles of daily life. We shall have to fight; our sword hand may never be at rest. We are besieged daily by the demons of hatred and pride, despair and fear. Love of God, love of humanity—don't these words sometimes have a dreadful irony when we utter them? But what reason have we to think that the love of God should be easy? The Paschal liturgy speaks of a merciless duel fought on the cross between Life and Death, Love and Rejection. It takes a strange passion, a strange patience, to learn to love as Christ loved us.

With a great patience

Indeed it is this word "patience" which flows naturally from St. Paul's pen when he sings his hymn to love: "Love is patient and kind" (1 Co. 13.4). By patience we are to understand that spiritual strength which renews itself in silence and love. The soul will not let its patience be exhausted. It bears everything with Christ, and with him experiences, unexpectedly, fresh impulses of life: "We are treated . . . as dying, and behold we live" (2 Co. 6.9).

In the midst of this world which God so loved (Jn. 3.16),

the mark by which Christians are distinguished is this: "By this all men will know that you are my disciples, if you have love for one another" (Jn. 13.35). This is how the power of the gospel is made present to the world.

23. Wise as Serpents and Simple as Doves

This is what our Lord said when he sent his apostles out into a threatening world: "I send you as sheep in the midst of wolves" (Mt. 10.16). And therefore, he tells them, they must be "wise as serpents and simple as doves." Strange words to show us how we are to travel and to strengthen our hearts on the way. They are especially helpful for us, who must live in the world as men of the gospel.

Wise as serpents

Why should a serpent be offered as a model? Certainly not because of the guile he is credited with in Genesis, where it is said that the serpent was more subtle than any of the other creatures made by God. Nor because of a certain wicked cleverness in getting out of a predicament, like that of the dishonest steward (Lk. 16.8).[1] No, it was rather because he moves so fast and never lets himself be caught by surprise. He is alert and wise.

[1] We know, of course, that in this parable the steward was not praised for his *dishonesty* but because, in the worldly sense, he was *prudent*. It is as if our Lord were saying: "Ah! if only you had as much shrewd sense where the kingdom of heaven is concerned as you have in worldly affairs!" But this is another meaning.

The exact words used in this text are enlightening. The Greek word applied to the serpent is *fronimos*, which means alert, sensible or wise. As we know, in the Bible the word "wise" does not mean simply knowledge of something we have read or been taught, but knowledge gained by living, experiential knowledge. In the Bible the wise man is he who has an interior sense of the things of God; the unwise man is one who has lost this sense and so is adrift in the world. Thus St. Paul says: "Have this mind among yourselves, which you have in Christ Jesus" (Ph. 2.5);[2] or, more tersely, "Feel as Christ felt." We understand better now in what the wisdom of the serpent consists, why he should be offered to us as a model—we have only to look at him! We can see that he will never be caught by surprise; his senses are alert for danger, and he is sharply aware of everything about him. So is the Christian who has the mind of Christ. In the midst of this difficult world what will be his guide? His sense of the mind of Christ—surer, more demanding, but also less rigid, than all his reasoning.

The gospel theme of watchfulness enlightens us in the same way. We know how our Lord asked his apostles to "watch" —that is, to remain awake when so many things invited them to sleep. The parables of the "wise" and foolish virgins (Mt. 25.1–13) and of the "wise"[3] and the wicked servants (Lk. 12.45–48; Mt. 24.48–51) describe the situation people find themselves in when they take the chance of falling asleep and are surprised by the Master's coming. For when the Lord finds us not watching for him, but befuddled with sleep, he will

[2] The Vulgate reading is: "*Hoc sentite in vobis quod et in Christo Jesu*": "Let this mind be in you, which was also in Christ Jesus."

[3] Again the same word, *fronimos*.

say, as he did to the foolish virgins: "I do not know you."
This truth will shine out on the last day: Blessed is the servant
whom the Master finds "watching," the one who has guarded
an awareness of Jesus in the depths of his soul. But it shines
out daily as well; for Christ's comings are a daily occurrence,
and only those who preserve recollection in the depths of their
souls, those who are "watching," recognize him. "I say to all:
Watch" (Mk. 13.37).

The disciple of Christ is not deluded by false prophets or
antichrists. Let us not pretend that these are only to come in
the last days of the world: their presence is a reality for all
times, hence of ours. "Beware of false prophets who come to
you in sheep's clothing, but inwardly they are ravenous
wolves" (Mt. 7.15). "Take heed that no one leads you astray.
For many will come in my name, saying, 'I am the Christ,'
and they will lead many astray" (Mt. 24.4–5). "For false
Christs and false prophets will arise and show great signs and
wonders, so as to lead astray, if possible, even the elect" (Mt.
24.24). In the midst of such events, confusion in doctrine and
all kinds of turmoil, is it so easy to keep one's head? always
to be able to discern whether it is Christ or not Christ? Comfort, money, leisure, progress, ambition, skill, science, culture
—is it Christ or not Christ? Who will tell us? And Christ
answers simply: "Be wise as serpents and do not sleep."

St. Paul says to us: "Feel with Christ,"[4] or "be wise in
Christ." In one sense this simple sentence says everything. If
we could look ahead from the point of view of Christ we

---

[4] Always the same word: *fronein.* The force of the term "in the
Lord" is evident. It is a question of a total renovation of the judg-
ment. We must, in everything, have "the mind which was in Christ."
Such is Christian prudence.

should see our way much more clearly, and he would not let us dash our foot against a stone. But we do not learn such wisdom in one day: it takes our whole life, and often suffering, too. But we are not left without help, God himself gives us this sense of Christ. It is present in us through sanctifying grace and through prayer. It is our guideline, and we can lose it only through our own fault. It is our part to follow it faithfully every day. Every day we increase in human wisdom as we learn to see the world as it is. Every day too, we must grow in the wisdom of Christ by learning to see the world in our Lord, to see it as he sees it. "Be wise in the Lord." "Brethren, do not be children in your thinking; be babes in evil, but in thinking be mature" (1 Co. 14.20).

The disciple of Christ who wishes to live according to the gospel in the world must constantly refer to this sure sense guiding him. Here is his light: "Be wise as serpents"—that is, "Be wise in Christ."

Simple as doves

It is obvious, after what we have been saying, that this second part of Christ's teaching does not contradict what has gone before: it is rather essential to it. It is only by being simple as doves that we can be wise in Christ. The supreme wisdom of his kingdom is found in the simplicity of a dove.

The word used here means "pure," "untouched" "simple." Doves were felt to be without malice, they represented integrity and fidelity. Christ requires that there should be no trace of duplicity in his disciples. In a world where so much is not what it seems, where the devil's game of double dealing (and triple dealing!) is the rule, Christ says to us: "Just say

'Yes' or 'No'" (cf. Mt. 5.37). Thus it is easy to see why the dove is to be our model: we must be as simple as doves. Is it possible to live in this world and keep our hearts unstained? Without grace, of course, it is impossible; but God calls us to a share in his way of acting. And we must intend always to choose Christ, even if in our human weakness we sometimes fall into the duplicities of the world as well. We cannot be Christ's disciples unless we have chosen a kind of behavior which consists precisely in being without ulterior motives. A man with a simple heart—what a force he is in the world!

We must not let ourselves be tainted by the spirit of the world, but always keep the spirit of Jesus and his gospel of love in our hearts. Who is the wise man, who does not allow himself to be deluded, but he who keeps an upright heart, simple and pure in the sight of God? In this all Christian "cleverness" consists.

"Let us, therefore, celebrate the festival, not with the old leaven, the leaven of malice and evil, but with the unleavened bread of sincerity and truth" (1 Co. 5.8). "Put away all malice and all guile . . . Like newborn babes, long for the pure spiritual milk" (1 Pet. 2.1–2). "That you may be . . . children of God without blemish in the midst of a crooked and perverse generation" (Ph. 2.15). "Your eye is the lamp of your body; when your eye is sound, your whole body is full of light" (Lk. 11.34). If we try to live these words, we shall discover what light and strength they give to us in our work. Christ does not deceive us: it is the innocent heart which sees clearly.

To bring this about, we must live in the presence of God, and remember that it is not we ourselves who make our hearts upright, it is God looking at us. The aim of the Sermon on the

Mount is to raise our souls to this height. We so easily live according to our own lights or "play to the gallery," but Christ teaches us to live in the presence of his Father, not looking at ourselves and worrying, but turned unreservedly towards him and the tasks he gives us. Only then will we become straightforward and innocent.

But as we go on our way among the great or small struggles we encounter in this world, we are not to be naive. We must be mature in Christ. We shall win nothing by adopting the devil's weapons; we must use our own, those which Christ gives us, the arms of purity and truth. If we must cross swords with anyone, it will be face to face. And our fight will not be in vain: Christ says to us: "Be of good cheer, I have overcome the world" (Jn. 16.33).

Nothing is impossible to God

The gospel phrases are so clear and simple, but to a superficial view they are so remote from experience that one is a little discouraged, perhaps, when one hears them. How is one to live by them? Indeed they would be discouraging if no more were involved than a text; no more than words—sublime, to be sure, but transitory. But infinitely more than a text is involved. These words are Christ himself present through his Holy Spirit. It is to Christ, then, that we must turn. He it is who strengthens our hearts, patiently, all our lives long. As he said to the apostles, so he says to us: "Behold, I send you out as sheep in the midst of wolves" (Mt. 10.16). And he sends us out armed with his power.

Part IV
AT THE SERVICE OF THE WORD

24. The Word of God Is Living

The word of God is still living and mysterious as it was when the world began, and when the Church was founded, and so it will remain forever. We are told in Genesis that everything was created by the word of God, and the Acts of the Apostles tell us the glorious story of his word founding his Church through faith and baptism. St. Paul gives thanks to God because his converts received it "not as the word of men but as what it really is, the word of God," and he adds that it "is at work" in "believers" (1 Th. 2.13). And in our own days, in our parishes, in Sunday schools, missions, our homes, this almighty word still constantly nourishes and stimulates us. This means that our thoughts, our words, are no longer entirely our own: God constantly speaks in us and through us, and he says: "The kingdom of God is at hand." Let us play our part in the work of God's word.

All things were made through his word

This immense universe in which we live, so startling in its vast size, so baffling in its complexity to our small minds, is not meaningless. The patient work of scientists trying to understand its mysteries is not in vain. The eyes of faith must see the universe as what it really is—a word of God. As Aristotle said, long ago, "Things exist, and they cannot lie."

We who believe in God should listen, to hear them speak of him, for all things exist through his word. "And God said. . . . And God said . . ." is the constant theme of the account of the creation of the world in Genesis.[1]

St. John, in the prologue to his gospel, tells us that this word by which everything was created is a person—the very same Person who became flesh for our salvation: "All things were made by him." All things, but in a special way his creature man.

The story of creation is marvellously related in stone on the north portal of Chartres Cathedral. There, at the beginning of everything, the artist shows us Christ, already with his crossed halo. And when God, before creating man, contemplates him in his mind, he sees beside each other the face of Christ and, beautifully rendered, the face of man, made in his image.

It is because we are created through the word of God that we dare believe, in spite of appearances to the contrary, that man hears in his soul, secretly and persistently, a call to Christ, who is the light of his mind.

And what is created through the word is also created through the Spirit of love, who in the beginning was "moving over the waters," as a bird hovers over its nestlings. All the works of God tell us of his wisdom and his love; with his grace and the light of faith we can see in them the beauty of his word and feel the breath of his Holy Spirit.

If God has not revealed it to us,[2] it seems too daring to try

[1] On the theme of the creative word, cf. Wis. 9.1; Pr. 8.22; Si. (Ecclesiasticus) 42.15; Jn. 1.3; also the valuable reference and notes of the Jerusalem Bible.

[2] As, for instance, he revealed the significance of the human couple, the sign and the shadowing forth of the infinitely higher mystery of Christ and the Church (Ep. 5.25–33; Gn. 2.20–24).

to identify the particular end for which, if we may put it so, any particular detail of his creation was made. But we can be absolutely certain of the meaning of the universe in its entirety! It is an expression of his infinite wisdom and love. We shall not be misled if we listen to the psalms which sing the glory of God as it is shown in his creation: Psalms 8, 19, 104, for instance, and many more. And let us listen also to St. Augustine questioning creatures. "Speak to me of my God," he says; "tell me something about him. . . ." And he hears them cry out, "He made us!"[3] Listen to St. John of the Cross, a great mystic who was also a great poet:

> Rare gifts he scatterèd
> As through these woods and groves he pass'd apace,
> Turning, as on he sped,
> And clothing every place
> With loveliest reflection of his face.[4]

But let us also listen to those scientists of our time who are Christians too, but who speak in a very different idiom. They wish to sing of the glory of God, the one God who made heaven and earth, by means of the discoveries they make about his creation. In them, as in St. Augustine, the same faith seeks to integrate knowledge.[5] Faith tells them that the whole world,

---

[3] *Confession*, Bk. X.

[4] "Songs between the Soul and the Spouse," *The Complete Works of St. John of the Cross*, trans. by E. Allison Peers (Westminster, Md.: Newman, 1949), Vol. II, p. 443.

[5] We are familiar with the well-known dictum of St. Anselm: "Faith seeks understanding." Within the mind of the believer and within the mentality of an era there is a constant movement, either spontaneous or the product of reflection, in which faith strives to integrate itself with human knowledge, to the end of perfecting the human understanding which it indwells.

the universe, is made through God's word: somehow, they know, the world must speak of him.[6]

Go and tell my people . . .

But if God had spoken to us only by his works, we would still be in darkness. "The eternal silence of these infinite spaces frightens me," as Pascal said. But in fact, the Christian God, the only true God, has condescended to reveal himself to us, and has told us that he is interested in our hearts, if we may put it so. And he continues to teach our hearts.

Throughout the two thousand years between Abraham and our Lord Jesus Christ, God was forming his people with strength and patience. Today the Church still draws on the treasury of tradition assembled during those years. The God who called Abraham by his name and led him out of Ur of the Chaldees; the God who spoke with Moses in the cloud on the mountain; the holy God of Isaiah; the God of interior— as against exterior—justice of Jeremiah; the God whom the psalms show us as the God of the poor; this God is our God.

Within one people he raised up messengers with enlightened consciences, and through them he gradually revealed himself to his people. Little by little they began to see his face—that same face which our mothers, enlightened by Christ, taught us to recognize; the face which the Church always holds up to us, and which, in another way, his grace unveils in our hearts. In the light given to us by Christ we find him in the

[6] The endeavors of a Father Teilhard de Chardin, for instance, come to mind. Whatever may be the final judgment of his work, his effort and the meaning of his effort are shedding much light—that is, the integration of faith with the vision of the scientist.

psalms and in the writings of the prophets; through them he speaks to us.

In other words, sacred history teaches us that the word and the Spirit came to certain men and made them messengers and prophets.[7] These men were usually involved in the collective history of Israel: in fact God used both words and events to reveal himself, and each throws light upon the other. The exodus from Egypt, the entry into the promised land, the exile and the return from exile, and at last the destruction of Jerusalem—all these have a meaning. Through them, God was revealing himself, his word taught the hearts of men through each of these events. He speaks to us through history.

Even today, the same law applies. It is true that with the coming of our Lord Jesus Christ the face of God is unveiled. No messenger, no event, can add anything really new. And yet we do need time and history so that we may come to understand these things better day by day. The Church tries in a thousand ways to educate us in this way, and in our own personal history we must learn what God wants to teach us— through human love, the birth of our children, our trials, sorrows, even faults. For it is through this visible pattern in our lives that the one God reveals the face of his justice and mercy to our hearts.

In the case of the collective history of humanity, we must learn what God wants to teach us through the numberless appeals which come to us from the whole world, from the tall apartment houses in our suburbs all the way to those far-

---

[7] Read, for example, about the calling of Abraham (Gn. 12): of Moses (Ex. 3); of Jeremiah (Jr. 1.4–10); of Isaiah (Is. 6). Compare these with the callings of John the Baptist (Lk. 3.2–3) and St. Paul (Ac. 26.12–18).

off countries threatened by famine. Here again the Church guides us in our search. She speaks to us through her utterances and messages, teaching us that the living God, the only revealed God, is concerned for us in our distress, our wanderings and our faults: telling us what it is that he is constantly saying to us.

And the word dwelt among us

As we write these lines we are already—as you certainly know—bathed in the unique light which comes from the Son of God. We know how St. John, in words of majesty and tenderness, announces in the prologue to his gospel and in that of his first epistle: "That which was from the beginning . . . which we have touched with our hands concerning the word of life . . . we proclaim to you . . . that our joy may be complete" (1 Jn. 1-4). Now God has at last revealed his face completely. He who wishes to know him need only look at his Son: "This is my Son, my Chosen, listen to him!" (Lk. 9.35).

In order to hear God, then, we must listen to Christ. And how does Christ speak to us? Above all by his example. We shall never finish meditating on his life, his humiliations, his prayer, his forgiveness, his love, his cross and his glory. His words move us to the bottom of our hearts: his words as they are written in the sacred text of the gospel, words made living and effective through the power of the Holy Spirit. And there are his saints, living examples of the power of his word in the Church, with their testimony of fraternal charity, his sign par excellence of the authority of the truth in their hearts and of the power of Christ shown in their work. And finally, there are all those messengers of his, his priests, to whom he gave authority over his flock, and all those other members of his body to whom also he has given the mission of proclaiming that the kingdom of God is at hand. We hear Christ speaking to us in all these different ways.

And we know his ways: he dwelt among us. St. John uses an extraordinarily strong word to express this: "And the word became *flesh*" (Jn. 1.14). He chose this way so that he might be able to speak with us, and he completes his teaching only at the end of our life on earth. The Word of God did not use the abstract language of philosophy: he became flesh in order to speak directly to our hearts. And so that we might hear him even when our own flesh is crucified, the Word was stretched on the cross from which he teaches us in silence and love. These are the ways in which God spoke to us through his Son. This is how we too must speak to our brothers if the word of God is to reach them.

And they were filled with the Holy Spirit

Under the Old Law the word of God reached only a few privileged souls. But since the passion and resurrection, all men can become members of the body of Christ, and the whole body drinks of one Spirit (1 Co. 12.13). Where does the word of God dwell now? It dwells in the body of Christ. All who are part of this body share in the Spirit and the word. By their rebirth in Christ they are "spiritual" and "prophetic" —that is to say, animated by the Holy Spirit of love, and urged on by him to speak of God in word and deed.

On this earth the sign and standard, so to speak, of the body of Christ and his kingdom is the visible Church: the Church of all the baptized, the hierarchy and the faithful forming this one body. It is the mission of this visible Church to announce to the pagan nations that the kingdom of God has come, that it is here, close at hand. All its members have a part in announcing this, each in his own place, the hierarchy alone having authority, on which the faithful depend; but for all the members the same Spirit bears witness.

Those who are called the laity are not silent partners: the Spirit of God dwells in them too, and bears witness through them, as it does in priests and religious, although in another way. The human and holy success of Christian homes, the hospitality of a Christian couple, the courage in loneliness of a single man or woman, the silence of consecrated lay life, patience in trials, the faith of a catechist, the work done in an active household, the thinking of intellectuals, the united prayer of the Christian assembly—God lives and acts through all these.

Through all of them God's word reaches the hearts of men and brings light into their darkness. For to all the word continually retells the extraordinary Good Tidings which we sometimes hear in our hearts and which our lips declare in a great surge of joy: God is Love.

25. Saved by the Word

God continues to speak to us throughout our lives: he speaks to our hearts. Moreover, his word not only teaches us, it takes hold of us, changes us, converts us—it *saves* us. We shall try to explain how this is: first, on the personal plane—God's word addresses itself to the depths of the heart; second, on the institutional plane—God's word is uttered through the Church founded for our salvation.

The illumination

The Word of God became flesh and dwelt among us: he was a tangible presence in our midst. The essential, decisive words he pronounced entered the heart of men, where they will remain forever, working like leaven. On the cross he became the supreme Word of Reconciliation, and now that he has ascended to the Father, he continues to intercede for us. It is exactly true that he is the Word who saves us.

But it is important for us to understand how this is done. It is not done mechanically and without our having any part in it, but by means of the light of Christ and the voice of his truth, which touches our hearts. This may be an aspect of redemption to which we do not pay enough attention: God saves men individually by speaking to their hearts. St. John and St. Paul repeat this constantly—the word of God saves us by "enlightening" the eyes of our hearts (Ep. 1.18), by making eternal life manifest to us (1 Jn. 1.5–7). Remember St. John's light-darkness dialectic. Without light in his soul man is a prisoner in a world in which he understands nothing, a prisoner in the closely barred cage of self. This is human isolation in darkness which no ray comes to lighten: sin. Here indeed he enters a dark night; not the star-filled night of God, nor the cloud of dark knowledge which is so painful to the intellect and yet give peace. No, this is "darkness" in the strong sense the word has in Scripture: spiritual death. When the light has gone out of man's heart, he sits in the shadow of death.

But listen to St. Paul: "For once you were darkness, but now you are light in the Lord" (Ep. 5.8–14). What a cry of deliverance! Not only do you *have* light, you *are* light, "light in the Lord." And this is the hymn that used to be sung over the newly baptized:

> "Awake, O sleeper, and arise from the
> dead,
> and Christ shall give you light" (Ep. 5.14).

This is the salvation brought to us by baptism. It is not given mechanically, as if we were made of wood, but spiritually, through light, as befits spiritual beings and the living God who loves them: "And Christ will shine on you." We know how insistently the Fathers speak of baptism as the sacrament of illumination. The soul, the *mens*, of man—the heart of his mind—which was in darkness, which *was* darkness, is now full of light. Christ has become its light: its sun in the word of God which enlightens every man who comes into the world. The word is in his heart, it dwells in him and enlightens him: "He who hears my word . . . has passed from death to life" (Jn. 5.24).

How do we receive this saving word of God?

In baptism of course, but also through faith. St. John and St. Paul keep telling us so. Faith, as we read of it in the Scriptures, is something very different from obeying certain conventions, or from a purely intellectual adherence to principles, however necessary this may be. It is a matter of our whole being welcoming God and his word. And to do this we need a humble and adoring heart which believes, submits itself to the divine words, even before they are spoken: like the child Samuel falling on his knees and saying: "Speak, Lord, your servant is listening." It is not a question of the word of God suiting itself to us; on the contrary, it is we who must let ourselves be converted through it.

When the grasp of faith is almost total, the word of God can convert us at one stroke, as St. Paul was converted on the road to Damascus: the word penetrated to his heart and transformed him for life. More often, however, conversion is slow: God seems to need our whole lives to complete it. But his pedagogy follows the same essential laws in either case. He lets one of his words fall into our hearts: a phrase from the gospels, perhaps —"Go, sell all you have"—or some word from his Church; a meeting with a friend; an encounter with someone in whom we see the image of God; or, often enough, the experience of the cross—that word like a two-edged sword; or the gift of his joy. This "word" then becomes for us a ray of divine light, a call. If we are faithful to it, it will make its way in us and finally convert us. But unfortunately the parable of the man who "went out to sow" still describes what can happen to the word: perhaps the ground of our hearts was stony, with little earth: the word endured for a time and then withered away. The light which had begun to grow in us was extinguished and we plunged back into darkness. But, thank God, it is true too that there is still good soil where the word yields a hundredfold.

Let us pause here for a moment. Many Christian men and women have days of recollection and retreats. Every group has one of its own. In these retreats the word of God is heard with joy, perhaps even with eagerness, but what real fruit for God does it produce in the end? We priests, too, faithfully make a retreat every year: we keep silence in the presence of God, we pray, we listen to his word—and yet how slow we are in being converted to him! Why is this? It is one of God's mysteries, but at least it is always good for us to have to confess that we are poor sinners! But what is the reason, really? After all, God's honor and his kingdom are at stake. Why is conversion so slow? What do we lack? Let us read the gospels again and we shall find that we need these things: a deep fidelity in "keeping" the light that converts us burning in our hearts, a refusal to be distracted by trifles, total abandonment to his grace, a fundamental docility to the ways of God, courage and perseverance.

All this is impossible without grace. But the word of God is not simply a light showing us the good but leaving us powerless to attain it. It is a call from God and a presence: the presence of Christ who can do all things. Our Lord himself said: "The words that I have spoken to you are spirit and life" (Jn. 6.63). Animated by the Holy Spirit they become life for the soul. They convert it, and what seemed impossible becomes possible after all. Then man sells what he has. He looks at

Christ and follows him. Herein is his peace: "If you continue in my word, you are truly my disciples, and you will know the truth, and the truth will make you free" (Jn. 8.31–32).

The Church and the word

But the word of God is not only a divine light in our hearts silently urging us forward. The word has been spoken audibly by the Word Incarnate. It continues to be heard in and through the Church, which was instituted for our salvation. Set up among the nations she never ceases to call them to come to the saving truth.

Perhaps we are not used to seeing the Church in this light, as the Holy Church of the Word of God. Yet that is what she essentially is. First, because she was founded by the Word Incarnate. The same God who created all things through his word conceived her in his wisdom from all eternity. Christ on the cross called her into existence and she was born from his pierced side, as the story in Genesis relates that Eve came from the side of Adam. She is truly born of his word, "cleansed by the washing of water with the word" (Ep. 5.26). More intimately still, she is, of her essence, the Word of Salvation sent forth among men until the end of the world. As Christ is the Word of the Father, so his Church is that same Word present among us. Even in "the Church of Silence" she remains the Church of the Word of God. "Woe to me if I do not preach the gospel," said St. Paul. The Church would no longer be the Church if for an instant she ceased to proclaim the word of God.

We know that she does this, first, by announcing the truth that saves us. Every unbeliever in good faith should have an opportunity to hear this. If he goes into a church, he should not leave it without some of Christ's light having reached him, either through his eyes or his ears. If he enters into conversation with a Christian, he should afterwards feel more quiet and more readiness to listen in his soul. Throughout, from the hierarchy to whose care she is entrusted to the laity—in all her members, in fact—the Church is the Church of Truth: that is to say, she is at the service of Christ's truth: "He who hears you hears me." Moreover, she possesses the words which sanctify, the sacramental words. She says: "Your sins are forgiven," and they are forgiven; "This is my body," and it is Christ's body. Finally, she commands and governs: she leads the flock to the pastures where they can nourish themselves on truth. Her laws are not given to increase our burdens but to protect us from evil. Sometimes, when there is danger, she must even threaten.

Thus, whether in the intimacy of our hearts or the public domain of the institutional Church standing in witness among the nations, the word of God saves and never ceases to save.

Dear readers, may you hear the saving word and receive it into good soil in your hearts. And may you be, for your unbelieving brothers, a true sign of the Word which can transform their darkness into light and their sadness into joy.

26. Servants of the Word

In the prologue to his gospel, St. Luke uses a remarkable expression: he speaks of "those who from the beginning were eyewitnesses and ministers of the word" (Lk. 1.2). What a unique privilege they had! We ourselves were not eyewitnesses, and yet God calls on us, too, to do our part as servants of his word. How can we, laymen, do this? We shall try to suggest an answer in this chapter.

The Word of God, a mystery and a reality

To our modern way of thinking, the term "Word of God" is perhaps not immediately clear: it may even sound abstract and impersonal. "Person" or "presence"—the person of Jesus, the presence of God in our lives—means more to us today.

But the Word of God is truly a presence and a Person: "Word" even adds one of his fundamental characteristics— he is a presence that speaks, the mystery of a person who reveals himself to us. The God who reveals himself, the Christian God, is a God who speaks to his children: "In many and various ways God spoke of old to our fathers by the prophets; but in these last days he has spoken to us by a Son" (He. 1.1–2). He still speaks to us in other ways too: through his creation, through the reality of the things he has made, through events in the lives of individuals and of peoples in which he is chief mover, through sacred history and Holy Scripture, through his Church and through the Holy Spirit. As soon as we "hear" God speak our hearts are filled with light and joy.

And he speaks to us continually: the mystery of his word is always living and active. We need not search for it in archeology or in history or exegesis (however essential these may be): we have only to believe with a living faith that God acts at this very moment, that he is speaking to us now, that he is inviting us to cooperate with him in the building up of the body of his Son—again, at this very moment. Our everyday life brings us into contact with a visible world, very real and solid, made up of people and things. But at the same time we know that there is something else beyond what we can see, something closely related to the visible world. There is God, there is Christ, and the mystery of his grace—and his grace is not a hidden, impersonal force. It is God speaking in the depths of our hearts, and making use of all creation to do so. His word goes forward unceasingly among us, enlightening us and calling to us: "O that today you would hearken to his voice! Harden not your hearts . . ." (Ps. 95.7–8).

Now we must understand that God draws us on, his believers, to cooperate with this living mystery of his word. We are not doing so if we are content to be silent under the pretext that it is none of our business to speak, for God has deigned to "need us"—he really wants our help. But we are not doing it either, if we never stop talking and working, for this is above all, God's "business" and his mystery, not ours. So we must pray continually: then, with all our confidence and all our courage, dare to speak when our words are really needed: "Speak and do not be silent . . . for I have many people in this city" (Ac. 18.9–10).

Let the word of Christ dwell in you abundantly

This is the advice St. Paul sends to the Colossians (3.16). How many of them were there? Surely not very many: and yet in this first assembly of brethren the word of Christ was living and active. St. Paul wishes ardently that it may dwell in them and bear abundant fruit. This means that the body of the faithful will become the body of Christ, the dwelling where the all-powerful word of Christ, living and active, will abide.

We know the Catholic doctrine on this point. It is in the whole mystical body, hierarchy and faithful—each in their own sphere—that the word of Christ dwells and—if we can put it that way—draws the breath of life. Only the twelve apostles, with Peter as the first among them, have the official authority to proclaim the word to the world; the other members of the body may proclaim it only in union with the apostles and under their guidance. The body of Christ thus "hierarchized" is a mystery where the word of God is guarded as the earth holds the seed, or better, as a mother guards her child. Therefore, no Christian can truly say "Jesus is Lord!" (1 Co. 12.3), except through the Holy Spirit and in continuity with the twelve apostles.

More concretely, every one of you, Christian laity, if you are baptized and confirmed, are part of the body of Christ, and as such become, whether you wish to or not, witnesses speaking for—or, alas, against—his presence and his word. The Holy Spirit who manifested himself at Pentecost in tongues of fire bears witness in you that Jesus still lives, that the kingdom of God is at hand, and that there is in heaven a Father watching over his children. The word of God lives in you and the Spirit urges you on to proclaim through your life, your prayer, your words and your silence that there is more to reality than the things that can be seen and touched—that God and his Son Jesus Christ really exist. And what the Holy Spirit urges you to give witness of, the twelve apostles, in their turn, give you the specific mission to proclaim. Listen to what the hierarchy of the Church has always said to you and still says, perhaps with even greater urgency, now in our times: "Go forth, bear witness, proclaim everywhere that Jesus is the Lord." Has the immense effort of Catholic Action any other aim than to awaken the resources you have in you through your baptism and to set them in order for the preaching of the gospel? God's word lives in the laity too, and presses you to speak out in your own way.

Servants of the word

How are you to be, in your own way, servants of the word of God? One fundamental condition is to be integrated not only with the Church but with the people among whom you live. This takes place first of all by baptism, which makes us able to take part in the Church's mission and its treasure; for even though you may not have been given any particular mandate, by the very fact that you are baptized and confirmed you have been commissioned by Christ and his Church to be witnesses of God and of his kingdom. Moreover, there are various mandates which the Church does entrust to you. In one way or another, lay people are an integral part of the Church, but it is just as important that you are an integral part of the world of men—your brothers. This is what gives meaning to the vocation of the layman. He is in the world like the leaven in the dough, like the seed which falls into the earth and dies to bear its fruit. The concrete human conditions of life: everyday occupations, the world of work, commuting, life in huge apartment houses, leisure, human joys and sorrows—all these can be food for God's grace. And if the layman is not thoroughly immersed in all this, who will be? In the conditions of her daily life Mary of Nazareth was a woman like any other, the difference was in the incomparable way in which she listened to God and dwelt on his word.

The same holds true for a layman who wants to be, as God asks of him, a servant of the word. What would he have to say —whatever his eloquence—if the word did not dwell in him? How could he be the leaven in the world, if God did not give him from moment to moment the supernatural vitality of the gospel? In order to "speak" in the name of God, we must first, and often, be silent and listen. Listen to whom? To God who speaks to us through all creation, but especially through his Church, and the cry which goes up to him from the depths of our brothers' hearts, even though they may not yet know by what name to call him. Constant reflection, the sometimes anxious search for the right words, for an opening through which God may reach the hearts of our contemporaries: these are part of our silence. Who does not know that evangelization requires—perhaps more than ever, today—a Christian penetration of other cultures, other civilizations, other mentalities, and that even a beginning cannot be made until we truly understand them? How can they understand us if we do not speak to them in their own language? The language of the human heart may be unchanging, but it is influenced by all that people see, touch, hear at this present moment. What Christian apostle, working among today's human masses, has not cried out to God in his distress, asking for the gift of tongues?

After listening to God, a man can speak in his name. How?

First through the testimony of his life. Few things are as demanding as this. For if the testimony is to be convincing, there must be no dishonesty. Yet who among us can say that he does not cheat unconsciously in his interpretation of the gospel? God knows this, and yet he accepts our service. But he requires that our hearts should increase in purity, little by little; in other words, that we must be determined not to cheat consciously. We are only poor men, and we do not try to conceal this: we are "just like everybody else," and so others will listen to our testimony, because we are really trying not to be pharisees. And sometimes, perhaps, God accepts our efforts, even without our knowledge, just because we are so dissatisfied with ourselves. When we meet an honest man—disinterested, ardent, generous, patient under trials—doesn't this make us reflect seriously on our own behavior? This is the testimony of example: it sometimes succeeds when words have failed, for it causes us to search our hearts.

Besides giving testimony when they can, laymen are often asked for advice on all kinds of matters. This is especially their province, in which they can be involved in a way particularly their own. When they have achieved a certain maturity and position in life their advice may be sought not only in trifling matters but concerning serious, sometimes crucial, decisions: tragic family problems, household crises, questions on the education of children. What are they to say? They cannot refuse to give an opinion: they must enter into "the counsel of God." It is their business, at such a moment, to be servants of the word. Who does not remember having called, sometimes in

anguish, for God's light, so that he would not say just anything, but exactly what God wished him to say, and what his
brother needed to hear? What sort of Christian layman could
answer such a request by saying that his brother's problem is
no concern of his?

There are also situations which occur in all our lives occa-
sionally, where a layman must take a stand, say what his conscience commands, speaking without affectation or bluster,
but without fear or timidity either: these are times when he
must openly profess his faith. Of course this does not happen
every day, but it may occur more often than we would suppose. There are simple words, spoken out of a deep conviction, that one must have the courage to say when they are
required, whether at a meeting, among friends, on a com-
mittee, or anywhere else. In such cases a layman need not be
afraid—a sincere faith, a firm conviction expressed simply and
firmly, without pretension, is always respected. This also is
cooperation with God's word.

Finally there are many more specific lay activities in the
service of the word, and this seems increasingly true nowadays. The collaboration of Christian laymen with the press
and other modern means of communication which influence
our contemporaries' mentality is increasingly daily, as it daily
proves more necessary. Moreover, such collaboration in this
field is a criterion of the vitality of the Church. If only priests
speak and write, it is impossible to know whether the Church
has really taken root in the world of men. But it is only too
evident that this active collaboration of the laity means that
they must become experts in their field. And that so many have
done so is a sign of the truth which fills us with happiness.

Collaboration of the laity in the transmission of the faith

is even more necessary: a vast number of projects for the teaching of doctrine are springing up. As with any serious work, catechetics, however modest the scale of the undertaking, requires training. The most indispensable part of this is, of course, the living assimilation of the faith by the catechist, but we must not forget that the gifts of the Spirit are many and that the body is not well served if all its members are trying to do the same thing. So one may have received the gift of hospitality, another visits the sick, another is involved in the social struggle, but all participate in the mystery of the word. Each of us must consider what God wishes him to do where he has placed him, and what his special grace is. But all the same, he must listen anxiously to the call of the millions of children waiting to be evangelized. The priests are overwhelmed—so many great apartment buildings, and more and more children in them waiting to hear of our Lord! And besides the children, there are adults just discovering—or rediscovering—God who must be taught about him in their own language, the way of speech they understand. Who will instruct them? What Christian homes will provide them with godparents?

Christian lay people, can you still say that you have no part to play in the mystery of the word of God?

27. The Word Is Born of Silence

Every true word springs from silence. Silence is the earth in which it was nourished, its living matrix. We know the famous formula attributed to St. Antoninus, "Silence is the father of preachers." We would like now to consider this profound law.

True silence

Let us first eliminate that evil silence which consists in a proud retreat into oneself in bitterness, hardness, indifference. This is the opposite of fruitful silence: it kills communication, it is a kind of death. Beyond that, there is another kind of silence which may still be impure—that in which a man is seeking, rather than giving, himself: this is the too humanistic silence of art, culture, natural contemplation. Let us think instead of true Christian silence: the silence of a soul led by God to go outside itself, to live and breathe in the presence of God, in true love. This silence is full, fertile, positive. It is fitting for a soul engaged in speaking with God and finding in him the source of all its other words.

It is always difficult to discover where, in man, this silence springs from. One way of putting it is to say that there is in each of us a pair of inseparable parts: the part that acts and the part that listens. The first anticipates, organizes, fights, struggles, and it is important and necessary. The second, more mysterious, part, while it also organizes, anticipates, struggles, is not completely absorbed in these things. It meditates on the deep realities of things, and listens to God himself, simply but supernaturally. There is silence in our being when we are not completely absorbed in our activities and when this deep part of our soul is listening. You know how our Lord spoke of this in the Beatitudes. Blessed, truly blessed, according to him, is he who throughout the struggles of this life hears the word of God and keeps it. This part of us that listens is neither a myth nor a creation of our imagination: it really exists, a creation of God, and lives in us with sanctifying grace.

This is how St. Thomas, with his usual precision, tries to define this part of our soul that listens. He distinguishes two functions of our unique human intellect, a practical or active function and a speculative or contemplative function. The first is directed to creating order within man himself and the material world in which he lives. Whether mechanical skill and the making of tools is involved, or the virtue of prudence exercised in the ordering of one's own life or the lives of others, it is this first function which comes into play. The second function is ordered not to the organization of matter but to communion with reality itself: it "knows," and in this knowing reaches its term. The first function is well developed in men of action and is, of course, indispensable. The second belongs rather to contemplatives, and in a sense it is even more indispensable. We use the practical function to plan, to organize our lives, our profession, our household. We use the speculative function when we pause, listen, communicate in our minds with the profound realities of life. Silence in our lives is not simply the result of following a formula, it goes deeper than that: it is the fruit of a steady, day by day, faithfulness to our contemplative function.

It is through charity—real supernatural love—that the Christian structure of our minds is formed from within. It persuades us to work for God—to plan, organize and struggle for him. This is charity in its active function, and there can be no saints, no holiness, without it. But charity also informs that deep part of the intellect whose role it is to listen: this is its contemplative function. For before action, charity must come into being, draw the breath of life, grow, wait. And even during action, if we preserve the recollection which is the life-breath of charity, it will mean a growth in contemplation. Thus the area of Christian silence widens in our lives to the extent that we are faithful through charity in living close to God.

Lastly, it is God who causes this silence in us, and fills it with his presence. Such silence is opposed to the kind of busyness in which the soul sees itself as its own object and center. Just the contrary is true: the soul's detachment from itself is the measure of the extent of its silence. We do not need to concentrate on creating silence in our souls, we only need to love God and speak to him often. It is he who fills our silence with his presence, and this is our salvation: we do not have to live alone with ourselves, we live with God. And when traditional Christian spirituality uses such phrases as "retire into yourself" or "live in your heart," these are perfectly accurate words, but they are only an invitation to leave the noise and superficiality, appearances and pretenses of the world, in order to make our home in the Reality which God is. Listen to St. Dominic: he wanted his brothers to speak with God alone, so that they would be able to speak about him.

The word is born of silence

Now we begin to see why all true words can only be born of silence. It is because silence is not just emptiness but the vital center of the soul. What happens in this vital center depends on what kind of subject enters and fills it. If the mind is filled by a really great subject, the soul pauses to contemplate it, and keeps silent. It is alive and profoundly fertile. If the subject is small, narrow, untrue, the soul is filled with confusion and noise and can neither listen nor speak. Thus it is the quality of the subject filling the soul which conditions its response: silence or speech. You may know Saint-Exupéry's lovely phrase, "The space in which the spirit can open its wings is silence."

And this is very true: but you can see that for a Christian it is also ambiguous, because everything depends on the quality of this "space." It may be only the space of our own mind, our own depth—always limited, and in the final analysis no greater than we are ourselves. But through grace it can be the space and depth of God, and this is an entirely different matter. That silence which is the father of the words spoken by a Christian is the silence which is of God, silence filled with God: the kind of silence, therefore, that is attentive to everything that comes from God, and to everything that is waiting for God. Not just any word is born of this silence, but a word from God. This is just another way of saying that it is already a great help when a mind is naturally deep: it will fly from noise and distractions, for instinct tells it that true life is not to be found in them. Yet in the end everything will depend on what it has found to nourish it, on who dwells in it. "He must increase and I must decrease" gives us a hint of the way we are to go. When we have dropped out of sight and God has taken the whole space in our hearts—and this is what charity tends towards—then our souls will enter fully into the silence of God, and quite spontaneously they will utter a word of God, a word about God—probably without knowing it.

How can a layman live this law?

There are only a few things we want to say.

The more we overexert ourselves, the noisier our lives unfortunately may be, the more necessary it is to keep and nourish in our souls a "point of silence." Everything in the desert changes when water is found. Around any source of water life is reborn: living water is well named: it brings life. So it is with our souls; noise makes them sterile, ruins them. If we can keep a little spring of silence in our hearts, they will revive every day. Of course there are some rhythms of life which are destructive to our souls: these we must discover and fly from at all costs, but there are also revivifying rhythms to be discovered and sought out. But the first necessity is to keep this simple, unifying spring of silence which unites us to God and helps us to receive everything from his hands in strength and peace. This is the one living cell from which our spiritual life constantly revives.

Of what is this simple and living "point" made? It comes from a complete surrender of ourselves into the hands of God and a state of prayer in which we rely entirely on him, and if he should give us the gift of contemplation we shall gaze at him with great faith, great love and complete abandonment. This "point" can remain in us in spite of struggles, anguish or even times of utter darkness. Let us repeat—this "point" is no invention: it really exists. God constantly creates it in us by means of sanctifying grace. Let us dare to believe in it, defend it, nourish it.

Thanks to this area of recollection we can keep our souls safe in God's hands. It is thanks to it also that we can listen to our brothers. A large part of life is made up of technical or utilitarian work which we can attend to with accustomed attitudes or reflex actions. If this was all we had to do, a clear, methodical, well-organized intelligence would be all we needed. But another part of our life is concerned with human relations, where we are dealing with other people—each of whom is an intelligent, free, spiritual center, with his own mystery. At this level a single, clear, technical mind is hopelessly insufficient. We need a mind that can be silent and listen, a love willing to receive love; and here also silence is needed. Only if we can be silent can we listen to our brothers —marriage partners, children, friends, employers, employees —and really hear what they are saying to us. Otherwise we are always too busy to hear what they are really saying when they try to speak to us: too busy with our own concerns, our preoccupations, our personal worries—all our "noise"! Then we do not know either how to listen to them or how to answer them with true, meaningful words, born of silence and charity. This is probably the reason for many meaningless lives in which there is so much misunderstanding, and such harmful loneliness: there is not enough silence in them. When God asks us to speak to our brothers it is implied that first of all we must keep silent and listen. Does it often happen that we do?

A great part of apostolic activity lies in the testimony of our lives. The ancients even raised example to the level of a *cause*. Good example builds up the body of Christ: it is one form of the word of God. But experience teaches us that our lives will only be heard as words of God if we ourselves speak with God. Charity, strength under trials, patience, magnanimity—all these come from the silence that unites us to God. Our closest neighbors, our companions at home, at meals, at work—what do they hear from us of God, except for this silent word, the testimony of our daily life?

To counsel a brother is an important part of the apostolic activity of the laity. A layman may be asked for advice on serious human problems more often than a priest or sister. If he is, it is his own true and very real manner of being a servant of the word. But clearly, if his counsel is to be discreet, attentive and respectful, his soul must habitually contain this "point of silence" of which we have been speaking. A troubled brother will speak only if he senses in the listener a silence full of concern, even of love.

The same could be said about the spiritual works of mercy: the grace to understand and comfort—in the sense of strengthen—a man who is being sorely tried. What word of comfort can ever be born of anything but silence!

Lastly there is the doctrinal ministry of the word in its many forms: catechism, catechesis for adults, doctrinal writing, etc. Here again, the same law holds good: the word of God is born of silence. We cannot teach it until we have been seized by its mystery, and this can only happen if we listen in silence. What grandeur is ours—is it really possible that God entrusts his word to us, and that we are to teach it to someone baptized in the name of the Father and of the Son and of the Holy Spirit—this same God, already so close to his soul and to ours?

CONCLUSION

28. The Disciple Took Her to His Home

Do you see what solemn, reverent emotion appears in St. John's account of the crucifixion? Live again the scene he relates so simply and with such awe: "Standing by the cross" —a cross on which a man sentenced to death was in agony— "were his mother, and his mother's sister, Mary the wife of Clopas, and Mary Magdalene. When Jesus saw his mother and the disciple whom he loved standing near, he said to his mother, 'Woman, behold your son!' Then he said to the disciple, 'Behold your mother!'" And John concludes simply: "From that hour the disciple took her to his own home." This was the hour which counted most in his life. At our baptism we also were given Mary to be our mother—when the time comes, may we too "take her to our home"!

Behold your mother

St. John seems to have been specially chosen to manifest this aspect of the mystery of Mary, by which she is our mother, the mother of the faithful. Yet St. Luke had already suggested it, when he presented Mary as the "daughter of Sion" who embodies, and indeed surpasses, the expectation of the people of God. He shows her as the type of the Church, which is at the same time her mother and her daughter.[1] And if Mary represents the Church in an eminent way, does not that also make her a mother in a wonderful manner?

But it was left to St. John to make her motherhood explicitly manifest. To be convinced of this, we must understand the way he writes.[2] Like a delicate artist, he suggests more than he actually says, or rather we might say that his writing is on two planes, historical and symbolic. He relates real historical facts: the marriage at Cana, the cure of the man born blind, the miracle of the loaves, the piercing of Christ's side, for instance; each historical fact is at the same time a sign with a spiritual meaning. Cana symbolizes the Church; the man born blind comes from darkness and is given sight by Christ, the light of the world; the miracle of the loaves symbolizes the Eucharist; the pierced side of Christ, the mystery of the sending forth of the Holy Spirit and the birth of the Church. If we do not see the spiritual significance in these events (which St. John stresses), then we shall not understand what he wants to teach us.

So it is with what he says of Mary, mother of the faithful. There are only two places in his gospel where John speaks of "the mother of Jesus": Cana and Calvary. Notice that these

---

[1] In his admirable narrative of the annunciation, St. Luke, in the manner of a biblical writer, clarifies the scene he describes by placing it in the context of scriptural tradition. Thus he sees clearly in Mary the one who incarnates, while wholly transcending, the "daughter of Sion" who is awaiting the Messiah (Lk. 1.28; cf. Zech. 9.9; Zeph. 3.14). The Magnificat is not only the personal canticle of Mary but that of the community of the faithful awaiting the salvation of Israel. Moreover, Mary, the mother of Jesus, explicitly mentioned as being in the Cenacle, watches over the newborn Church (Ac. 1.14).

[2] With reference to this entire chapter see Father Braun's beautiful book Le Mère des Fidéles.

two scenes mark off the beginning (Jn. 2.11) and the end (Jn. 19.27–30) of Jesus' ministry. It is easily seen that Cana symbolizes the passing of the Old Dispensation—the symbols for this are the six[3] water jars intended for the ritual washing of the wedding guests—and the coming of the New Dispensation, signified by the wedding feast and the presence there of Jesus and his disciples (Jn. 2.1–2; cf. Jn. 3.29; Mt. 9.15).

When we come to Calvary, we see that according to his manner of writing, John unveils the mystery of the cross. The Lamb of God is stretched on the cross, and "not a bone of his shall be broken" (Jn. 19.36; cf. Ex. 12.46); from his pierced side come water, the symbol of the Holy Spirit and of baptism, and blood, the sign of our redemption; is it not the Church, precisely the Bride of the Lamb, who is born from his side? (Rev. 21.9; 19.9; cf. Ep. 5.25–32).

Now it is extremely significant that on both occasions, at Cana and on Calvary, each of which sheds light on the other, and on these two occasions only, St. John explicitly mentions the presence of Mary. "The mother of Jesus was there" (Jn. 2.1). "Near the cross of Jesus stood his mother" (Jn. 19.25). And in neither case is Mary unimportant, an extra. She is important; she even plays a leading role. At Cana it is at her request that Jesus advances "his hour," the hour of his glorifying passion,[4] making it a prophetic anticipation of the event:

---

[3] Six—that is, seven minus one—is the figure par excellence of "incompleteness." Doubtless this symbolism of figures is rather foreign to our modern mentality, but there is no question that it expressed something very real for St. John. We must take it into account if we want to understand him.

[4] St. John uses the expressions "my hour," "the hour of Jesus" to designate the event which gives the full meaning to our Lord's life and his mission—that is, his passion, through which he glorified his Father and himself also (cf. esp. Jn. 12.23; 17.1).

"This, the first of his signs, Jesus did at Cana in Galilee, and manifested his glory" (Jn. 2.11). Again on Calvary, Mary is there, and Jesus has a special message for her, now that his hour has come, the hour of his passion which is also the hour of the Church. Jesus said to his mother, "Woman, behold your son." Then he said to the disciple John, "Behold your mother."

Further light is thrown on the deep significance of these words for the Church by the way in which St. John refers to himself as "the disciple whom Jesus loved." Faithful to his own manner of writing, St. John leaves no doubt that by this term he means himself: a real historical person, John, brother of James and son of Zebedee, and at the same time the type of the "spiritual disciple." By this he does not mean to present himself as an "initiate," apart from the other disciples, but as the very type of the disciple Jesus loves, faithful to his vocation to the end—that is, always receiving and keeping the word (Jn. 1.12; 8.37; 8.55; 12.47, etc.); abiding in the word (Jn. 8.31); keeping the commandment of love (Jn. 13.34); knowing how to abide in Jesus and the Father (Jn. 15.4, 9, 10, etc.) in the midst of a world where everything passes away (1 Jn. 1.17). And it is to this disciple that Jesus entrusted his mother, proclaiming bonds between them which the Church was to realize and manifest more and more as time went on: personal, loving bonds between mother and son, son and mother.

As we said before, a careful reader of St. John's gospel will find it difficult to suppose that there is anything accidental in the manner in which he writes. We are not concerned here with abstract speculation but with the revealed word. John was given the mother of Jesus as a sacred trust, and he is teaching us that "the disciple whom Jesus loves" is the disciple who received Mary as his mother and takes her to his own home.

Mother of the child in us

Can we describe Mary's motherhood in more psychological terms, define what it is in particular that she gives us? The first thing to come to mind is that Mary is mother of the child in us—the child spoken of in the gospel, as when our Lord said: "Unless you turn and become like children, you will never enter the kingdom of heaven" (Mt. 18.3). This was said so definitely, and in such circumstances—he was speaking to the twelve he had called (Mk. 9.35–37)—that we must see in it one of the major teachings of Christ. It is not, of course, a matter of pretending to be children—"playing the child"—we must become children in the sense of relying entirely upon God and letting ourselves be led by him into the purest depths of the divine simplicity. It is always by means of this childlike attitude that God leads us. When Pope Pius XI canonized St. Thérèse of Lisieux he was not afraid to say that "spiritual childhood is one of the secrets of sanctity."

Now this is one aspect of our souls in which we are especially dependent on Mary, first because she is our mother, and it is a mother's task to bring up children—the smaller they are, the more they depend on her—and second because she is herself the perfect example of a child of God, virginal and pure, and relying entirely on him. That is why, in Christ's Church, to go to the Virgin is to become a child in the blessed sense of the word—as Bernadette of Lourdes did, Catherine Labourée and Thérèse of Lisieux. It is by no means the way of easy childishness, it is the path of those who are truly mature in Christ. And yet it is an "easy" way, the way of abandonment and love.

Mother of interior contemplation

Here again, we do not start with abstract speculation, we open the gospels. It is St. Luke who shows us Mary as the one who "kept all these things"—everything to do with Christ—"pondering them in her heart." It is St. Luke also who tells us who Christ said were truly blessed: "those who hear the word of God and keep it." Mary lived this blessing in a special way: she of whom so little is said in the gospels, but whose silent presence we feel throughout. It was not by chance that the disciple to whom Jesus entrusted her was the one of whom we read that at the last supper he was "lying close to the breast of Jesus," the one who had listened to his words so attentively and who repeats so often our Lord's insistence that we should "abide in him."[5]

There is nothing artificial, then, in saying that it is Mary's role in the Church to be in a special way the mother and guardian of contemplatives. Did not her special friends and confidants live in silence? Need we remind you again of Bernadette of Lourdes and Thérèse of Lisieux? At a time when everything conspires to distract us, how good and helpful it is to remember that Mary, our mother, still teaches us to love the better part, the way of contemplation which, as Christ

[5] The word "abide" is one of St. John's key words, used more than seventy-six times in his writings. It designates the faithfulness and the interiority of the love which abides in the beloved through all the circumstances of life. (See, among other references, Jn. 15, where the word is used ten times in seven verses.)

said to Mary of Bethany, "shall not be taken away" from us.
(Lk. 10.42)

Mother of faithfulness to the cross

It is natural to us to reject the cross, to distract ourselves
from the thought of it: we are too frivolous to live in sight
of it. But then we are avoiding Christ, and that will lead to
our avoiding our brothers. Mary brings us back to them, without making us feel that we must be sad.

She stood at the foot of the cross: she had not run away:
there was no distraction for her. She did not sleep while Jesus
suffered! Just to be there, with all the intensity of her faith
and love—this was the way in which she participated in
Christ's redeeming work, how she joined in suffering the pain
in which the Church was born.

She wants to mother in us that part of our souls which is
faithful to the cross. Few things are as difficult for us as this:
it is not a matter of feelings, or even of our will, but of grace.
Only grace can give depth to our souls, make it possible for
the word to find good soil to grow in, so that it is deeply
rooted, giving us perseverance. We must offer ourselves to
Mary, asking her to foster this part in us. Only then shall we
be able to face our suffering brothers and take our place in the
drama of the redemption of the world. Only then shall we
have a part in the fruitfulness of Christ and the Church (Jn.
12.24; 15.2).

Standing at the foot of the cross Mary suffered, but her
faith remained, and her hope. In faith, the dawn of Easter was
already breaking. On the day of Pentecost she was with the
apostles: with them she was filled with the overwhelming joy

of the resurrection: the ardent expectation of the coming of the Holy Spirit. And now, the Mother of Holy Hope, she leads us on towards he who is to come—"The Spirit and the Bride say 'Come!' And let him who hears say, 'Come.' " And let us too say, "Come, Lord Jesus!" (Rev. 22.17, 20).